Improving Employee Benefits

Why Employees Fail to Use
Their Benefits and How
Behavioral Economics
Can Help

Stephen Wendel

Longfellow Press
Washington, D.C.

Longfellow Press
2121 Ward Court NW #3
Washington DC 20037

Cover Design and Illustrations by Katie Palermo
Edited By Dustin Schwanger, Nicholas Greene (Twin Miracles Editorial)
An Artisanal Publication

Printed in the United States of America
First Edition: September 2014

Publisher's Cataloging-in-Publication data

Wendel, Stephen.
    Improving employee benefits : why employees fail to
use their benefits and how behavioral economics can help
/ Stephen Wendel.
    pages cm.
    Includes bibliographical references.
    LCCN 2014914456
    ISBN 978-0-9903602-1-6

    1. Compensation management. 2. Employee fringe
benefits--Psychological aspects. 3. Economics--
Psychological aspects.   I. Title.

HF5549.5.C67W46 2014   658.3'25019

ISBN: 0990360210
ISBN-13: 978-0-9903602-1-6

CONTENTS

PREFACE

Defaulting employees into a 401(k) plan can double the number of employees who save for retirement.[1]

Presenting the current state of an employee's finances as a simple 0-100 score can increase savings contributions by $600 in a month.[2]

New research in behavioral economics and psychology is helping employers approach employee benefits in new ways. Many of these innovative and highly effective efforts, like the two examples above, explicitly focus on employee behavior and the behavioral obstacles that employees face. By helping employees overcome those obstacles, employers make more efficient use of their benefit dollars and enable their employees to fully utilize their benefits.

This book is about how to apply lessons from behavioral science to help employees take action on their benefits. All too often when people *intend* to do something, they fail to do so. They struggle. They get distracted. They don't know where to start. For example, we've all known people who say they want to live healthier, but just don't take the steps needed to make that a reality. Researchers are coming to better understand the underlying mechanisms that block people

---

[1] See Nessmith et al. (2007).

[2] Based on a randomized control trial (a.k.a. A/B test) conducted by HelloWallet. See Balz and Wendel (2014).

from following through on their intentions and how to design more effective ways to overcome those mechanisms.

Over the last decade, there has been a tremendous explosion of research in behavioral economics and the larger behavioral research community, reflected in popular books such as Richard Thaler and Cass Sunstein's *Nudge* or Dan Ariely's *Predictably Irrational*. Within this research, there are hundreds of individual biases and heuristics that affect our decision making process. Social Proof. Loss Aversion. Peer Comparison. Defaulting. The Pain of Paying. This research is being applied in diverse arenas, from the federal government[3] to consumer "wearable computing" products such as the FitBit Flex and Jawbone UP[4] to medication-adherence programs.[5]

We've started to see these techniques make inroads into the HR world as well — especially with 401(k) auto-enrollment and the writings of a few notable leaders in the field.[6] But, to date, no book has provided clear, effective guidance to HR professionals on how to integrate lessons from behavioral economics in a systematic manner. In other words, how to move from interesting techniques that *might* work to a clearly defined and practical process for HR. This book fills that gap.

Here, we apply behavioral research to the needs of HR practitioners. We'll discuss the underlying research in behavioral economics and the psychology of judgment and decision making and what it means for plan design and communications. We'll also examine the future of HR and benefits, in light of the behavioral research and the rapidly growing pool of data we can gather about the employee benefits behavior. We'll then dive into the details of how to practically apply it: From how to design a benefits package to how to craft and deploy well-placed, effective communications for your employees.

---

[3] Subramanian (2013), http://swampland.time.com/2013/08/09/nudge-back-in-fashion-at-white-house/. See also the UK Government's efforts: https://www.gov.uk/government/organisations/behaviouralinsights-team.

[4] http://www.fitbit.com/flex; https://jawbone.com/up

[5] Volpp and Asch (2014); http://www.glowcaps.com/

[6] For example, Benz Communications and Towers Watson.

Along the way, we'll examine both the current state of *knowledge* in the behavioral sciences as it applies to HR, as well as the *methods* behavioral researchers use. It's important to remember that researchers have only started to cover issues of vital importance to employers and their HR departments. While there are many powerful lessons already, there is also still much undocumented territory. In this book, I present an approach practitioners can use to improve benefits outcomes, even when there isn't ready-made research with answers to their questions.

By asking the right questions about one's benefits programs and vendors, HR departments can effectively apply the same methods that behavioral researchers do and gain greater clarity into their employee population. That doesn't mean HR teams need to learn statistics — but rather a set of precise questions to ask, and guidelines on how to evaluate the responses. HR can leverage the power of the purse to rigorously evaluate benefit programs before signing a contract, and then to hold them accountable for their real *behavioral* impacts on employees.

In addition, by applying potent lessons from the behavioral sciences, and gathering solid data about the behavioral impact of benefit programs, HR innovators can more effectively meet the unique needs of their employees — to the benefit of both employers and employees.

Who This Book Is For

This book is tailored to the needs of **Human Resources professionals**: both practitioners in the field and senior managers. If you work on plan design, internal communications, program administration or evaluation, or if you're an HR leader with diverse responsibilities, you'll find tools you can directly apply in your work.

The first section of the book outlines a new, behavior- and outcome-oriented approach to benefits. It also provides a foundation of knowledge in the behavioral research.

The second part of the book dives into the details of benefits practice and is particularly geared towards practitioners in the field.

Senior managers can focus on the parts that are of most interest to them, but otherwise jump to the summaries entitled "A Quick Recap," available at the end of each chapter.

For HR professionals, this book will help you be more effective in your work and stand out among your peers with new skills. Specifically, it will help you:

1. **Understand** your employees' behavior with respect to their benefits and broader total rewards packages

2. **Design** more effective benefits packages by focusing on their behavioral IOI (*impact* on investment, whether it be for a financial ROI or for other goals)

3. **Evaluate** and hold vendors accountable for their impact on employee behavior

4. **Deploy** more effective benefits communications using behavioral economic techniques

The book is meant to complement your existing expertise as an HR professional and give you practical skills and knowledge for plan design and communication.

Even if you're not an HR professional, however, you'll find insights and value here. In particular, there are four other groups who will benefit from reading this book:

1. Corporate finance

The chief financial officer (CFO) and the finance department will be particularly interested in the sections on program evaluation and on demonstrating the financial and workplace impacts of benefit programs. This information helps provide a common starting place for discussions with the chief human resources officer (CHRO) and the HR team.

2. Other company employees

Benefits packages are ultimately about serving employee needs — employers want to attract good people, and keep those employees engaged and interested in their work over the long haul. Even if you are not in HR (or finance), this book can help you understand what goes on behind the scenes in your HR department, and the significant amount of time and energy that goes into selecting and delivering your benefits packages.

This book provides lessons from the behavioral sciences on how to ensure that benefits packages are what employees actually need, make them easy to use, and ensure that they deliver on their promise for employees. It can help you learn about the inner workings of your benefits, and why they are delivered as they are. Along the way, you may find this book valuable for its discussion of the behavioral research and why we *all* struggle to use benefit programs like gym memberships or savings plans, even when we have every intention of doing so.

3. Benefits consultants

HR teams are navigating a sea of new requirements, benefits options, and competing claims about how to best improve outcomes for their companies and employees. Benefits consultants are in a unique position to help HR teams plot a course forward, combining knowledge about the needs of a particular employer and its employees, with a broad vision of current directions and issues in the marketplace. The best benefits consultants can help companies determine which vendor programs are really worth the money and which are not, and demand rigorous evidence from vendors.[7] Benefits consultants also can play an important role in applying the behavioral techniques discussed here — especially by recommending intelligent defaults and automation techniques when appropriate, and identifying non-obvious obstacles to employee engagement.

4. Benefits vendors and brokers

I must be upfront — I have some harsh things to say about how some vendors and their brokers promote their programs, claiming ROIs that simply don't make sense and aren't borne out by the facts. In this book, I show HR professionals how to identify the most impactful programs in the vendor community — and the valuable

---

[7] This is, when serving as an impartial consultant and not as a broker receiving a commission for the sale of particular programs — regardless of their true impact.

services they provide — and how to avoid the others.

As a vendor in this space, you'll learn about the new, sophisticated standards of evidence that companies increasingly require from benefits vendors. For many vendors, that will mean moving away from participant surveys towards stronger scientific evidence, especially experimental evidence, to demonstrate the efficacy of your program. For vendors that are already leading the way, however, you'll find that this book supports and validates your efforts.

In addition, throughout the book we discuss detailed behavioral strategies and techniques that vendors can use to increase benefits usage among employees who struggle: from leveraging peer comparisons and competition to framing effects and loss aversion.

Expertise

In terms of expertise, readers do not need to have any prior experience with behavioral economics or other branches of the behavioral sciences; this book provides the necessary background and techniques. It also doesn't matter what size company you work with — the challenges of making the best use of benefits bedevil us all.

Before we get into the nitty-gritty details, let's talk a bit about how this book came about.

HelloWallet, Behavioral Science, and *Designing for Behavior Change*

I'm the head researcher at HelloWallet, and a behavioral social scientist by training. I study "product-mediated behavior change"— a mouthful that means I examine behavior change at scale: How technology products, ranging from slick mobile apps to simple emails or text messages, can help people overcome obstacles and take action in their lives. Currently I conduct research around financial decisions and benefits usage, in partnership with behavioral economists and psychologists around the country, to improve the impact of HelloWallet's products.

At HelloWallet, we build software that helps people take control of their finances and make better use of their employee benefits. We work primarily with Fortune 500 companies, providing our software to their employees. We help employees get out of debt, build a cushion of emergency savings, plan for retirement, and everything in between. We also help them better use tax-advantaged vehicles like HSAs and 401(k)s. For employers, we provide rich information and analytics about employee finances in the aggregate, helping employers make better benefits decisions.

In addition to being a for-profit company, we have a strong social mission to give back to the community. We partner with organizations like Goodwill Industries and the Iraq and Afghanistan Veterans of America to give our software away to families in need. We are committed to working with the academic community, as well, and disseminating what we learn to researchers and the general public. It's been my role at HelloWallet to work with our diverse population of members — from retail workers to investment bankers — to understand how to effectively engender action around their benefits and then spread those lessons far and wide.

In 2013, I wrote a book called *Designing for Behavior Change*, published by O'Reilly Media. In that book, I summarized the relevant behavioral research and the lessons we'd learned applying it as we built HelloWallet's applications. The book provides a step-by-step process for designing, building, and testing software products that use behavioral research to help their users take action. It describes how software teams can integrate behavioral considerations into their product development and quality assurance processes.

If you're familiar with *Designing for Behavior Change*, that's great. Here, you'll find some overlap on the underlying theory (especially in Chapter 2), but the bulk of the book is new. Either way, this book is self-contained, covering all of the background you need. If you find yourself developing software products, though, definitely pick up a copy of *Designing for Behavior Change*!

Unlike *Designing for Behavior Change*, this book focuses on behavior change in a very specific and important context: employee benefits. Here, I examine how HR executives and on-the-ground practitioners can understand and apply behavioral insights to improve the impact of their work. I draw on the research literature, on our experiences at HelloWallet with our highly successful financial wellness offering, and the countless informal conversations and formal interviews we've had with other practitioners in the field — at plan sponsors, benefits providers, brokers, consultants, etc.

At HelloWallet we're sometimes asked how someone can apply the scientific knowledge we've built internally to their own company and benefits package. In this book, I hope to answer that question. However, the book is not about HelloWallet. We'll use some examples along the way, but that's it. Instead, it's about how you can apply the same behavioral approach to your work.

Isn't Auto-Enrollment Enough?

By now, most HR professionals are aware of the tremendous impact that retirement defaults have on employee savings: By automatically including employees in their retirement program unless they elect not to participate, companies can double their participation rates. While the concept only became widely applied in the last decade, almost 60% of companies now have auto-enrollment in place for their retirement plans.[8]

401(k) defaults are the quintessential example of behavioral economics in the human resources world. They entail a small, simple change in how options are presented to employees, with an almost unbelievable impact on employee behavior. Intelligent defaults build on a core lesson in behavioral economics — that people naturally follow the path of least resistance.[9] In survey after survey, most employees want to save for retirement but they fail to actively do so. By making *saving for retirement* the path of least resistance (your

---

[8] See Arnold (2014) http://www.npr.org/2014/04/21/303683792/how-do-companies-boost-401-k-enrollment-make-it-automatic. The rapid increase occurred after the Pension Protection Act of 2006 opened up the doors to auto-enrollment through greater protections for employers.

[9] See Berman, Ariely and Hreha (2014) for a short overview of this and other core lessons in behavioral economics.

employer sets up everything for you unless you choose not to save), employers help workers meet their own goals without coercion. Auto-enrollment (with auto-escalation) is the single most powerful action that employers can take to boost retirement contributions.

Auto-enrollment, while successful, is only the tip of the iceberg when it comes to applying behavioral research to employee benefits. The reason is twofold:

1. Auto-enrollment isn't relevant or appropriate for most employee benefits, especially with an increasing buffet of employee-selected plans in consumer-driven healthcare and beyond. Throughout this book, we'll discuss retirement planning and the important role of auto-enrollment, but also look more broadly at the full range of benefits. Thankfully, there are other powerful techniques that HR professionals can use outside of the retirement arena, which we'll discuss in detail here.

2. Auto-enrollment, even when combined with other auto-features like auto-escalation and rebalancing, is a partial solution to employees' retirement challenges. As Steve Utkus, the Director of Vanguard's Center for Retirement Research states: "Automatic enrollment is an essential strategy for all Defined Contribution plans ... but it is a 'blunt instrument' in that it is not personalized to individual needs."[10] Auto-enrollment also doesn't help workers become *personally invested* in their retirement planning. Thus at job change, they frequently move out of retirement vehicles[11]; 401(k)s then serve as a high-cost, short-term forced savings vehicle.

So, we'll talk about how to use auto-enrollment most effectively, and other ways to use defaults to structure the path of least resistance. Along the way, we'll place auto-enrollment in the context of other approaches employers can use and how to select the right method for a particular benefits challenge.

---

[10] Uktus (2014).

[11] Fellowes and Willemin (2013)

Well, How About Incentives Then?

Like 401(k) defaults, most HR professionals also have encountered — if not already implemented — a second major technique: the use of targeted incentives to encourage employee action on their benefits. As with 401(k) defaults, incentives are tremendously powerful in the right context, but limited in their scope. Again, the reasons are twofold:

1. Incentives are best suited for one-time actions. When employees are incentivized to do something, they usually continue doing it only when the incentive is explicitly applied. That's fine if you want them to complete a wellness survey, for example. However, the survey's incentives aren't relevant or effective if you expect them to exercise each day. Either continued incentives, which can get very expensive, or a different approach is needed.

2. Incentives can be inefficient. Especially for repeated actions like exercising, saving for the future, and eating healthy, direct incentives may be *effective* but not *cost-effective*. When employees face obstacles to using their benefits (as they generally do), it's wiser and cheaper to simply remove those obstacles, rather than paying employees to individually search for a way to overcome them.

Later on, we'll discuss the best use of incentives in detail, and show the costs and benefits of them versus other techniques for particular benefits contexts.

The Ethics of Employee Behavior Change

401(k) auto-enrollment, incentives, and many other behavioral techniques raise important issues about what's ethical and appropriate to use with employees. We can't avoid these issues, and it's better to confront them head on, so we can judge what is appropriate for a particular company and context.

In particular, we must ask ourselves:

> *Is it right to encourage employees to act in a certain way, like using a benefit program?*

Behavioral techniques are sometimes referred to as "nudging" — providing people with a relatively gentle push in a particular direction, especially when that direction appears to be in their interest.[12] These nudges give people the option to choose otherwise, but still explicitly encourage them to take a particular action. They have been employed in diverse ways — from encouraging recycling[13] to improving medication adherence,[14] and have been greeted with everything from delight[15] to horror,[16] especially when implemented by government agencies and omnipresent companies like Facebook.[17]

However, we "nudge" each other and ourselves all the time: We change the environment to encourage an action, without seeking to convince or coerce. We send our spouses text messages to pick up the kids on the way from work. We hang our keys by the door so it will be easy to find them in the morning. In fact, over the last decade, behavioral researchers have extensively studied simple

---

[12] See the aptly named book, *Nudge,* by Thaler and Sunstein (2008).

[13] Shunk (2009a) http://www.autoblog.com/2009/10/14/video-fun-theory-part-2-vw-makes-throwing-stuff-away-fun/

[14] Lowenstein et al. (2007)

[15] Shunk (2009b). http://www.autoblog.com/2009/10/08/video-volkswagen-wants-you-to-have-fun-taking-the-stairs/

[16] Lott (2013). http://www.foxnews.com/politics/2013/07/30/govt-knows-best-white-house-creates-nudge-squad-to-shape-behavior/

[17] On Facebook, a significant controversy erupted over their manipulation of members' New Feed Items based on their emotional content. E.g., Goel (2014). Another controversy occurred shortly afterwards when OK Cupid posted a remarkably poorly-presented blog entry about its own experimentation (see Rudder 2014), though often for good purposes, and testing that their software worked (see Hern 2014). For a longer discussion of the ethics of these tests — and how we have sought to apply ethical standard and avoid such controversy — see Overly (2014).

intuitive interventions like these, including straightforward text message reminders.[18]

Companies also nudge their employees, as a necessary and normal part of business. Effective nudges include everything from guardrails that protect workers from accidents on the job to open enrollment communications that carefully lay out the options for employees. So how can we carefully but pragmatically think about the behavioral techniques discussed here?

I think about behavioral techniques, and when they can be applied ethically, in terms of three factors: why, how, and who.

1. **Why are they doing it?** If someone pushes another person to do something they wouldn't otherwise do, and the person pushing directly benefits from it — that (rightfully) makes us uncomfortable. If they do it to help the person, that's better. If they do it to help the person *and the person asks for help* that's generally ok.

2. **How are they doing it?** The method matters. If we point a gun at another person and say they have to do something, even if it's in their own best interest, that makes most of us uncomfortable. But, if we present a choice and make it easier for people to act, that's generally OK.

3. **Who is doing the nudging?** In the US, our unease with nudges is strongest with government agencies, but we also feel it at lower levels with companies, strangers, and lastly, friends and loved ones. When employers try to encourage their employees to do *anything,* it can be risky. As Americans, we are (rightly or wrongly) skeptical of the motives of private companies.[19]

---

[18] See Karlan et al. (2011).

[19] Across all of these questions, there's an additional quirk of our society — if a lot of people do it, or it's been done for a long time, it's generally considered OK, regardless of the who, the why, and the how. Whether we like it or not, we accept things that have been around a long time. It's considered perfectly normal to dock an employee's pay for not showing up

Thus, private companies start at a disadvantage in one area — simply because they are private companies — but can and do apply nudges that are generally welcomed as appropriate and good for employees. For example, 401(k) defaults are generally accepted and normal, as are wellness programs in which employees are encouraged, but not required, to participate.

At the same time, companies are *expected* to look after their employees and to set up benefit program that will attract, retain, and otherwise help them. Helping employees is *why* so many people enter the HR profession in the first place. Further, if a company's benefits aren't used, they aren't "benefits" at all — they are a waste of time and money. So, companies already encourage their employees to use their benefits, with internal communications, benefits fairs, competitions, etc.

The result is an odd, and potentially very frustrating, situation. Employers are expected to offer benefits that people actually use. Unfortunately, employees too often say they want a benefit, but don't actually use it, or fail to devote the appropriate time and energy to get the most out of the program. On the other hand, employers need to be careful about how they go about encouraging benefits usage; like it or not, many people will presume the worst of companies — and their HR departments — if they consciously attempt to shape employee behavior.

Despite this odd situation — the need to support employees but the concern over doing so inappropriately — there is a path forward. In my own work, I seek to follow these guidelines:

❖ Tell employees what you're doing. If you're trying to encourage retirement savings, say so. There's no reason to hide it.

❖ If employees object, stop altogether or give them an *easy* way to opt out. Don't assume you know what is best for everyone. The company may have additional insight and

---

for work. But, increasing the cost of an employee's health plan for smoking is very controversial.

expertise into benefits challenges, but it's still up to individuals to determine what is right for themselves.

❖ Look for areas where employees want to take action but struggle (i.e., where they choose to do something, but face an obstacle and stop). In that way, the company best aligns with the interests of employees. Focus on ways to use behavioral research to facilitate and empower employees.

❖ Keep in mind that perception matters as well as reality. If people believe you are manipulating them, even if you're not, they'll be angry. When using a "new" technique from the behavioral sciences, it's especially important to be transparent, and work to *facilitate* instead of coerce.

Together, these guidelines set up situations in which HR aids employees to achieve their own goals — helping them become healthier, manage risk, take care of their families, etc. It also means avoiding situations in which employees would feel manipulated and would rightfully be angry.

There might be a good argument to be made for HR *pushing* people against their will to do something, like stopping smoking. But, persuasion and coercion are inherently tricky for employers to ethically handle, and that is not our goal here. For example, we will not discuss how to punish employees who fail to attend a wellness program with higher healthcare premiums.[20] Instead, these guidelines are intended to focus our attention squarely on areas of mutual voluntary benefit.

I strongly believe that employers can use behavioral techniques in ways that employees and employers can benefit, and that seem natural and normal. That doesn't mean that anything is fair game — instead it requires clear red lines to help everyone agree on what is acceptable and what is not.

---

[20] See bswift (2014); according to their survey, in 2014, 77% of large employers (>500 employees) provided incentives for health risk assessments, and 62% applied incentives for wellness education or classes.

The Chapters Ahead

Here's what you can expect in the coming chapters.

Section 1: Applying Behavioral Research to Benefits

Chapter 1 introduces the core premise of the book: Human Resource professionals can increase the impact of their work, and their company's benefits, through a targeted, research-driven approach to helping employees take action on their benefits. It describes how to examine employee benefits from a behavioral perspective, looking at the specific choices and actions employees face, thinking holistically across benefits silos, and assessing programs for their true behavioral impact. This approach builds on the vast body of research in behavioral economics and the psychology of decision-making, and complements the existing skills and expertise of HR professionals.

Chapter 2 teaches readers the central lessons of cutting edge behavioral research, as they pertain to employees and benefits. It describes key research studies and themes in the literature, then presents a straightforward model for remembering the cognitive preconditions for employee action: cue-reaction-evaluation-ability-timing-experience (i.e., CREATE).

Chapter 3 discusses how the *methods* used in behavioral research can be applied to benefits: specially, how to weave behavioral insights throughout the process of plan design and delivery. It offers six stages at which to use the research: analyzing, crafting, testing, implementing, observing, and navigating (ACTION) the use of "benefits interventions."

A benefits intervention is any change to a benefits package, whether it be adding a new program, changing the cost structure of an existing one, or redesigning communications employees receive about their programs.

---

xv

Chapter 3 (and the book) approaches benefits interventions holistically, looking for the right level and type of intervention that best solves an employee benefits challenge.

Section 2: Benefits & Behavioral Research in Practice

In this section, we walk through how to practically apply each stage of the ACTION model, step by step. Chapter 4 digs into the first stage, analyzing employee and employer needs, to determine the right behaviors to facilitate among employees. It discusses how HR practitioners can clarify their corporate and employee goals for benefits offerings from a behavioral perspective.

HR professionals have six strategies they can employ as they craft benefits interventions: defaults, financial incentives, channel factors, promotion campaigns, education campaigns, and changing the core benefits lineup. Each has its strengths and weaknesses in terms of driving actual usage by employees. Chapter 5 describes what each of these areas entail and the options available to the HR team.

The next chapter, Chapter 6, focuses on a fundamental question HR practitioners face when crafting a new benefit program: Will it actually work? The chapter discusses how to evaluate the evidence for a proposed program, whether it is provided by a vendor or developed in-house. There are common errors (intentional or unintentional) in how benefits providers test the impact of their products and present the results; this chapter provides HR professionals with the tools they need to determine where the data are solid, and where they are not.

Chapter 7 is about testing assumptions in a proposed change to benefits plans before it is enacted. We apply methods from the Lean Startup community to "fail fast": finding problems early, before they are expensive (and embarrassing) to fix. We also discuss how pilot programs are often ineffective as tests, because they come too late in the process, and take too much time and energy; ideally, testing benefits assumptions should be inexpensive and rapid.

Chapter 8 starts off a series of three chapters about the details of implementing benefit programs. In particular, Chapter 8 talks about the value of benefits communications. It covers how effective communications spur action, and how we should break free of the old the "big bang" approach to rolling out programs. Instead of big bang rollouts, it describes how HR teams can test and learn as they implement a program — providing greater value and impact for employees and their companies. That approach is known as "experimental optimization".

Even the best designed program can suffer from low usage. In Chapter 9, we dive into detailed behavioral tactics that HR teams can use to facilitate usage among employees. The chapter discusses how to identify the particular behavioral obstacles that employees face. It then offers a wealth of tactics from the behavioral literature, such as loss aversion, peer comparisons, social proof, and subtle framing effects, and discusses the scenarios in which each is most appropriate.

Chapter 10 focuses on the most important form of benefits communications for most companies — email — and how to leverage it to help employees take action on their benefits packages. We'll talk about the ins and outs of email subject lines, sender names, calls to action, and message timing. We'll also consider ways to satisfy the legal constraints and requirements that benefits communications are often under, while still engaging employees and innovating.

Chapter 11 wraps up our discussion of the ACTION model by discussing how to quantitatively <u>observe</u> the progress of a benefit program in action, and how to <u>navigate</u> the inevitable challenges that result — despite early testing and iteration. It covers the data you'll need from your IT team or vendors, and how to evaluate them.

Section 3: Wrap-up

A common goal for benefits packages is to increase "engagement". In Chapter 12, we take a special look at what "engagement" really means, and how benefits packages fit in. Unfortunately, engagement is often a vague concept, and the data around it can be confusing and contradictory. We cover how to measure engagement, what causes it, and how plan design (and communication) can help.

Chapter 13 concludes the book with a brief summary of the behavioral approach to benefits, a review of the practical techniques taught in the preceding chapters, and a vision of how behavioral research might shape and improve employee benefits in the years to come.

ACKNOWLEDGEMENTS

This book would not have existed without the help and support of my colleagues at HelloWallet. I am especially indebted to Aaron Benway, Arielle Cote-Colisson, Lee Eliav, Andrea Franklin, Lacey Herchek, Grant Karsas, Daniel Mazmanian, Katie Palermo, and Rob Pinkerton.

In addition, many kind people have shared their experiences applying behavioral techniques in the workplace or otherwise offered their suggestions along the way on how to improve the book. My gratitude goes out to Tom Armani, Gene Baker, Jennifer Benz, Christina Bishop, Rachel Bridges, Jeremy Citro, Amy Cribbs, Carl Cudworth, Charles DeSantis, Marco Diaz, Ken Fairchild, Melinda Grosskopf, Slaveya Ivanova, Jacob Jaskov, Scott Kirschner, Catherine Ott-Holland, Zander Packard, Brad Paz, Lynne Prescott, Matt Regan, Barbara Renterghem, Tim Riley, Cameron Sepah, Michael Siepmann, Greg Tahvonen, Katie Tierney, Jennifer Turgiss, Steve Utkus, and Philip White.

For Luke

SECTION 1:
APPLYING BEHAVIORAL
RESEARCH TO BENEFITS

1

A BEHAVIORAL APPROACH
TO BENEFITS

An increasing focus on consumerism. A growing array of wellness benefits. Crushing increases in healthcare costs. New investment options and rules. The HR environment is changing, and Human Resources professionals are being asked to rapidly adapt to these changes. There are new benefits offerings to vet and implement, new data to interpret, new laws and regulations to comply with and communicate to employees, and the ongoing need to make it all happen within tight budgets.

The benefits landscape is radically different for employees as well. Some of these changes are a consequence of developments within HR departments: Employees are being asked to set aside money for their retirement and manage their allocations, manage health expenditures, and make difficult health insurance decisions.

Other changes arise from the evolving characteristics of employees themselves: Americans face increasing health challenges due to obesity, diabetes and related conditions.[21] At the same time America is undergoing a two-pronged generational shift with older Baby Boomers retiring (or wanting to retire but not being able to do so)

---

[21] Sharpe (2013)

and Millennials flooding into the workforce, each group with distinct benefits needs and experience levels.

In this changing environment, the foundational questions remain for HR professionals with respect to benefits:

❖ What benefit programs will attract, retain, and motivate my employees and help them in their daily lives?

❖ How should these programs best be rolled out and implemented?

❖ How do I identify and encourage those who need the programs the most to actually use them?

❖ How do I know if a program actually works as advertised?

When employee demographics, benefits requirements, and benefit programs are all in flux, how can employers manage that complexity and find the most effective programs for their populations?

There's no simple answer. Despite broad trends in the field, each employer's situation is unique, as is each employee's. With retirement benefits, for example, defaulting employees into a suite of target date funds and a standard contribution rate can work well for the bulk of employees, but leave others unengaged in their benefits and unprepared for their real retirement needs.

While there is no simple universal answer, behavioral researchers have developed tools to find specific and effective solutions. The same tools have been used in diverse contexts from Indian sugarcane farmers[22] to payday loan clients in New York City[23] to 401(k) participants.[24] In each case, they have found localized solutions that demonstrably help people engage with and handle complex decisions — not unlike those facing employees every day.

---

[22] See Mullainathan and Shafir (2013)

[23] See Innovations for Poverty Action's US Household Finance Initiative http://www.poverty-action.org/ushouseholdfinance/projects

[24] Thaler and Benartzi (2004), Benartzi and Thaler (2001)

In this book, we'll see how that approach can be applied to the challenges that HR professionals face with employee benefits.

Core Principles

A behavioral approach to benefits focuses, not surprisingly on employee "behavior" — what employees actually do with respect to their benefits. Benefit programs are only meaningful when employees take action, in small or large ways. Employees should do something differently because of the program, such as saving more, eating healthier, or managing risk more effectively. *Effective benefit programs entail changing employee behavior.* That doesn't mean coercion or even persuasion — it can, and it should, mean helping employees take action when they want to, but struggle; for example, when employees want to eat healthier, but aren't successful. Behavioral research provides insights and tools to design effective interventions that make it more likely for these employees to take action.

However, because human behavior is so complex and multifaceted, it's all too easy to focus on the wrong behavior, use an intervention that doesn't work, or believe that a program is working when it really isn't. Crystal-clear goals and metrics help drive effective behavior change, and create impactful benefits. Together, they can direct the benefits process, from the initial design to the final evaluation.

You can think about these two principles as two interlocking parts:

Principle 1: Benefit Programs Depend On Behavior Change.
Principle 2: Behavior Change Requires Clear Goals & Metrics.

The first principle focuses on employees, who are changing in some way, and the second focuses on employers, who set the goals and metrics.

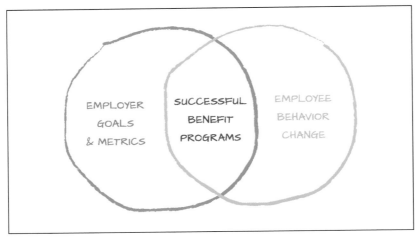

Figure 1: Impactful, successful benefit programs
help employees change their behavior toward some goal

At a 10,000-foot level, that's the **behavioral approach to benefits** we'll explore in this book. It's a simple and straightforward, but still quite unusual, way of looking at benefits. So, let's look at the two components of this approach in greater detail.

Benefit Programs Depend On Behavior Change

Benefit programs work best when employees take action: they depend on employee behavior change. At the most basic level, most programs are only effective when employees sign up for them or tailor them to their needs. That is, for a health insurance offering to be effective, employees should think about and sign up for the coverage that is appropriate for them. Or, for a retirement program to be maximally effective, employees should set the right contribution rate for their particular financial circumstances.[25] Often, a deeper and more lasting change in behavior is also important: such

---

[25] Auto-enrollment and auto-escalation are incredibly powerful tools that employers can use to *decrease* the work required of employees; but, as we'll see later, they are most effective when combined with positive action by employees: adjusting contributions to their needs, or opting-out altogether when appropriate. We're return to that topic frequently in this book.

as exercising regularly as part of a wellness program or taking medication for a chronic condition.

Without action on the part of employees, benefit programs will have little impact, regardless of the amount of time and money an employer devotes to them. The challenge is that employees have competing demands on their time: the default action is no action, or a perfunctory response, even when the employee needs and wants to use a program. Meaningful action on benefits requires a change in behavior.

We all too often assume that setting up a great program and telling employees about it is enough. Unfortunately, the data about employee engagement with their benefits tell us that it's not.[26] Even when employees sincerely *want* to use a program, many don't sign up or don't engage. The gap between intention and action is huge, for many reasons: Employees may not read the message announcing a new program; they may not connect it with the things they care about; or they may put if off indefinitely while attending to other tasks. Any of these situations is enough to derail an otherwise excellent benefit program.

In order to improve benefits impact, we need to carefully analyze the behavioral obstacles to action. Intuitively, we know some of the factors that underlie the lack of employee engagement. Employees aren't lazy or disinterested in their benefits, even though it might seem so sometimes. Instead, they are busy; they're stressed. At HelloWallet, we talk to users of our system who are simply struggling to juggle the needs of job, home, and family life — leaving no energy for planning for the future. We talk with others who have tried in the past to take control of their finances, but didn't do well, and now they carry that baggage with them — stopping them from trying again. In fact, a wide range of factors can block people from taking action despite their desire to do so.

Behavioral research can help us understand the particular behavioral obstacles that employees face. For example, employees may fail to act because of a lack of attention, relevance, or urgency. We're

---

[26] Gallup (2013a)

coming to better understand the underlying mechanisms that drive the gap between intention and action, thanks to research in the behavioral sciences. Popular books such as Richard Thaler and Cass Sunstein's *Nudge* or Dan Ariely's *Predictably Irrational* provide insight into the hundreds of individual biases and heuristics, such as social proof, loss aversion, and anchoring effects that affect people's decision making process, and whether or not they take action.

An understanding of behavior — and the obstacles that employees face — should infuse the benefits process from diagnosis and design to implementation and evaluation. When we communicate benefit programs, we naturally think about whether people will take action based on the communication. But, the message itself is only one of the ways in which we can support employee action.

We can tune the design of benefits to make *using* those benefits more likely for employees. Similarly, the small details of implementation are vital — behavioral scientists have shown time and time again how small frictions shape action. For example, setting the *default option* for employees on whether or not to participate in their retirement program has a massive effect on their actual participation. During the evaluation process, focusing on behavior and behavior change helps us better assess the true impact of the program, and determine how to improve over time.

Focusing on behavior change doesn't mean manipulation or coercion. Instead, it's about enabling employees to take action when they want to. All communications and design choices affect employee behavior — subtly or overtly. By focusing on that change in employee behavior, HR teams can more effectively support the actions that employees say that they want to take. The same psychological mechanisms that are used in sales and marketing to strongly persuade also can be turned around, and used for different purposes — helping empower employees to change behavior they already want to change. That is the focus of this book: How to design and deploy benefits to effectively support voluntary behavior change among employees.

Behavior Change Requires Clear Goals & Metrics

It's nearly impossible to help employees take action when you don't know exactly what you're asking them to do, or why. It seems obvious, but the implications are profound. Similarly, it's tremendously difficult to know whether someone takes action *because* of your help, or whether they would have done it anyway, without careful data analysis. Yet, too often we lack that clarity of purpose and objective metrics.

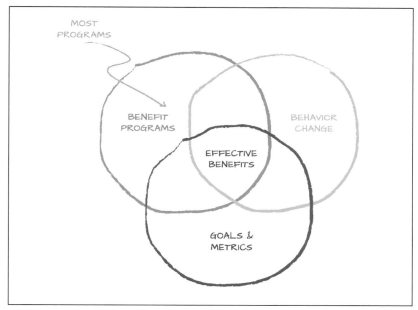

Figure 2: Unfortunately, most benefit programs lack clear goals and metrics, and don't help employees actually change their daily routines and behavior

Sometimes we shy away from hard-nosed metrics of success because we fear they might destroy the noble goals of helping employees. Or, because it's too complex to measure, and we fear that we'll lose sight of the human impact of our programs in the process. It's actually the exact opposite: We need hard-nosed metrics for our benefits to deliver on their promise to employees.

Once we start to apply that hard-nosed approach, we find all sorts of obstacles and inefficiencies that limit our ability to really improve the lives of employees. Hard-nosed metrics allow us to iteratively improve over time, and document that improvement — we don't need to be perfect on day one, but we can experiment and learn over time if the proper data tracking and assessment are in place.

A major obstacle to effective benefits is disagreement within the organization about what that impact should be! For example, consider retirement. At HelloWallet, we speak with a lot of companies about their retirement programs. What is the *intended* impact of a retirement program? Companies have diverse goals. For some companies, retirement programs are used to attract and retain talent; for others, it's a legacy contractual obligation that needs to be managed so as not to strangle the business; for others it's a way to ensure that employees can retire on time with a stable and secure future. Thankfully, disagreement can be uncovered early when you clearly define and measure their behavioral purpose.

For your particular company and your particular retirement program, you might pursue any one of these goals or many of them at once. But, if the HR team, the CFO, and, often, the employees themselves, don't know what the goal is exactly, then there's trouble. If there are unwritten rules or expectations of the HR staff that aren't fully shared and agreed upon, HR is put in a tight spot. If the reason for the existence of the retirement program is "because we need one," then employees and the company are being underserved.

Specific and unambiguous metrics of the impact of a program can have immense benefits to the HR team and to the company — namely:

❖ *Clear metrics settle arguments* among HR staff and between HR and the rest of the organization about the "right" approach to take.

❖ *Clear metrics facilitate improvement.* Once you can define and measure the impact of a program, you can measure potential changes, and know whether or not they improve outcomes for the employees and employer.

❖ *Clear metrics hold vendors accountable for their programs.* With a metric of success, you can require proof of impact upfront from a vendor and ensure that they live up to the agreement after the program is deployed.

Achieving clear metrics for benefit programs sometimes requires changing *how* we measure. All benefit programs help employees, and their employers, in some way. Putting a precise figure on that impact, and being able to judge whether one design is better than another isn't always straightforward. For example, if the intended impact of a retirement literacy program is to increase the retirement readiness of employees, then a survey of whether or not employees were happy with the program (something we come across all too often, unfortunately) misses the mark.

> *Unfortunately, most employee benefits surveys don't actually measure what is important: changes in employee behavior. It doesn't matter if people are happy with a program if they don't use that information in practice!*

In the research community, the gold standard for measuring the impact of a program is the randomized control trial (RCT) or *experiment.* In a benefits experiment, some randomly selected employees receive the program on day one, and others don't. Then, the company tracks outcomes for the two groups, and compares them. The random assignment process controls allows the company to look squarely at the impact of the program itself, and factor out any other influences — like the demographics of the employees, their prior interest in the program, their current habits, etc. It may sound a bit unusual, but the process is actually quite straightforward, and increasingly used by leading companies — and vendors — around the country.

HR professionals can more effectively evaluate programs beforehand, and hold vendors accountable afterwards, when they have a good understanding of experiments and other solid forms of evidence. Vendors often don't provide companies with the information they really need to understand the impact of a program. Companies are not being served properly if vendors try to distract HR with optimistic but vague or irrelevant numbers about the success of their programs.

However, how can HR really focus on creating a measurable impact when it is caught in the middle between employees and vendors? The middle is actually quite a powerful place to be. Think of HR as the gatekeeper. Vendors, and brokers, need HR to survive. Vendors want to serve employees, and of course be paid for their services, but they'll naturally only supply the documentation and evidence about their programs that is requested of them. Ultimately, it's the HR team that sets the standard and calls the shots.

At some HR events, though, it really feels the other way around — vendors circle around plan sponsors like sharks circling juicy prey. It's time that HR changes the game and starts being the sharks. HR teams can ensure that their vendors and brokers have the information and incentives they need to really support HR's benefits goals. But to do that, HR needs sharp teeth: a clear focus on impact, and a well-structured, unambiguous procedure for accountability.

However, an HR team doesn't get there overnight. It's a process that infuses how we think about the selection and deployment of programs. The same rigorous, thoughtful approach also underlies much of the best work in behavioral science: and it's what's behind the behavioral approach to benefits.

Being Focused Doesn't Mean Being Heartless: IOI Instead of ROI

It's important to remember that focusing on outcomes and behavior change doesn't mean the company isn't also focusing on the welfare of its employees. For many companies, the simple reason that a program exists is because "it's the right thing to do for our employees." That should be applauded, because that's the spirit of HR that keeps employees, and what's right for them, front and center.

However, having non-monetary goals does not mean that progress can't be measured. Whatever the goal is, the behavioral approach to benefits asks: "Are you striving towards the goal effectively?" Delivering a benefit program with the wholehearted aim of helping employees doesn't mean, sadly, that it is being executed as well as it could be. It doesn't mean that vendors are delivering on their promises, or that the program couldn't be adjusted to meet employee needs more effectively.

The behavioral approach to benefits, with its focus on goals and behavior change, does not dictate to employers and employees what those goals should be. This method can and should be used in cases where bottom-line financials are paramount, or where employee wellness is paramount, or even where simple employee satisfaction with a program is the primary goal of a company. As you'll see throughout this book, the approach we describe here is about making benefit programs more effective in support of the employer's and employees' goals.

The term ROI, return on investment, is often used to denote the purely financial benefits of an investment of resources, like a benefit program. Here, we use a broader term, IOI, for *impact of investment*. The true impact that the company's investment of resources has delivered, whether it be financial (ROI) or otherwise.

CREATE ACTION

Building on these two core principles, we'll examine the relevant research and guidelines for practitioners over the course of the book. We'll also use two mnemonics to remember the details of the behavioral approach: CREATE and ACTION. Together they show what is needed to help employees overcome obstacles with their benefits and infuse the process of plan design and delivery with clear metrics of behavioral impact. At the risk of being overly cute, they show what's required to CREATE ACTION.

The CREATE Model: Obstacles to Behavior Change

You can think about the cognitive prerequisites for action, and thus the obstacles that employees may face, with the acronym CREATE:

❖ **Cue:** Something needs to cue the person to think about acting.

- ❖ **Reaction:** The mind automatically reacts intuitively and emotionally.

- ❖ **Evaluation.** With conscious awareness, the mind does a quick cost-benefit analysis.

- ❖ **Ability.** The person must actually be able to act and know it.

- ❖ **Time pressure.** The person needs to have a reason to act now.

- ❖ **Experience.** The person generally needs to have a good experience the first time if they are ever going to (voluntarily) take action again.

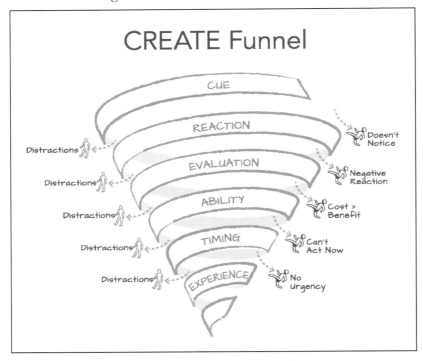

Figure 3: Six Obstacles to Behavior Change

The CREATE acronym comes from my book *Designing for Behavior Change*, in which I organized the research literature into these common lessons about individual behavior. In Chapter 2 of this book, we'll look at how those lessons apply to the specific circumstances of employee behavior and benefits.

The CREATE Model, and the larger behavioral literature behind it, helps to both diagnose the behavioral challenges that employees face, and find solutions. For example, simple reminders have been shown to be effective when our limited attention fails us. Creating specific intentions of when and how to act can help people overcome logistical barriers.[27] And, leveraging loss aversion and social proof can help overcome challenges of motivation. We'll match behavioral obstacles to the tactics that can help overcome them in Chapter 9.

The ACTION Model: Focusing on Behavioral Outcomes

At a high level, a behavioral approach to benefits isn't very different than what benefits experts already do — design, implement, and evaluate programs that meet the needs of their employees and companies. It's in the details that things differ, and behavioral research can provide additional insights that complement your team's existing expertise. You can think of the process in terms of six steps, from the initial assessment of the problem and crafting of the benefits offering to navigating challenges that arise post-implementation.

The process centers on benefits interventions: Changes made by the HR team that drive employee interaction with their benefits, whether those changes entail new programs, changes to existing programs, or more effective communication of programs already in place. Here is how those interventions are developed and deployed:

* ❖ **Analyze**: Figure out what employees need, given existing benefits offerings and the behavioral obstacles they face.

* ❖ **Craft:** Design benefits interventions that align employee and employer need, and help employees actually take action to use them.

---

[27] See Karlan et al. (2011) on reminders. See Gollwitzer (1999) on developing what are known as "implementation intentions".

❖ **Test**: Test key assumptions about the intervention before implementing in full.

❖ **Implement**: Implement the benefits intervention itself, tailoring communications carefully based on behavioral research.

❖ **Observe**: Assess the impact of the program with rigorous methods, especially randomized control trials.

❖ **Navigate:** Handle the inevitable challenges and find solutions; iteration is almost always required for effective behavior change.

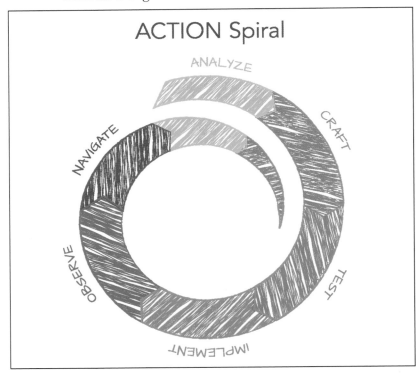

Figure 4: ACTION — 6 Steps for Integrating Behavioral Science into Employee Benefits

These two models, CREATE & ACTION can help you understand how employees make decisions (CREATE), and how to layer on a behavioral approach at each step of the benefits process and augment your existing process and expertise (ACTION).

A Quick Recap

At the end of each chapter, I'll provide a quick summary of the key lessons. That helps reinforce the concepts, and also can serve as a quick reference guide when you're in a hurry. Just check the end of each chapter to a get a simple, straightforward summary of what you need to know. Here's the quick recap of this chapter:

❖ The benefits world is in a period of great change, but many of the enduring concerns of HR professionals remain — especially how to select and deploy cost-effective benefits.

❖ At each stage of a traditional benefits process, there are tools from the behavioral sciences that can help empower HR to improve the impact of their programs.

❖ One core premise of the behavioral approach to benefits is that achieving impact entails behavior change — not sleazy manipulation, but helping employees take action. By systematically designing for behavior change, we can bridge the gap between intention (employees say they want to do something) and action (they actually do it).

❖ The other core premise is that professionals can and should keep a clear focus on the measurable impact of their programs. HR professionals should clearly define, design toward, and hold vendors accountable for the specific and measurable outcomes of their programs. The time for vague, feel-good data is over.

❖ We should check that the preconditions for employee action, represented by the acronym CREATE (cue-reaction-evaluation-ability-timing-experience), are all in place for our employees. We can overcome obstacles to action by applying behavioral science throughout the plan design and delivery process, represented by the acronym ACTION (analyze-craft-test-implement-observe-navigate).

❖ This approach doesn't mean losing sight of the core values of HR teams, however. It doesn't dictate a company's benefits goals — whether they be employee engagement or cost containment. It also doesn't entail coercion; benefit programs can only be effective in the long run when they are based on a transparent approach to helping employees take action on their own terms. That is what the rest of this book is about.

2

HOW EMPLOYEES DECIDE ABOUT THEIR BENEFITS

No one wants to get sick with the flu. But some people choose to get vaccinated, and others don't, right? In a breathtakingly simple and powerful experiment, researchers tested a mailer that went out to employees about their company's free, on-site flu shots.

In one version of the mailer, researchers added a simple suggestion: Write down the time and date you'll get the flu shot. They didn't try to convince anyone. They didn't even encourage them or give them information they didn't already have. They increased vaccinations by 12% just by providing that simple suggestion.[28]

As employees make decisions about their benefits, seemingly innocuous changes in the design and communication of those benefits can have outsized impacts on their behavior. We just have to understand the decision-making process.

Benefits are only effective when employees take action to use them. That's just obvious, right? Sure. But rarely do we systematically examine how employees decide to use them, or not.

Since benefits are only effective when used, one can naturally ask: Why would employees use them? We often think about employee

---

[28] Milkman et al. (2011).

behavior as something that naturally happens or doesn't — if employees really want to do something, they will. If they don't, they won't. If the program is "good," people will want it. Otherwise, they won't. Unfortunately, it's considerably more complicated than that.

"Why do people take the actions they do?" is a core question facing behavioral researchers. Researchers again and again show that we fail to do the things that would help us, and we even fail to do the things that we want to do and are able to do. However, there's an odd sort of logic that our minds follow as we make decisions. Thoughtfully designed benefits interventions — whether they be emails to employees, posters in a break room, or fitness campaigns — can leverage that knowledge to help people take action.

While each employee is different, our brains are fundamentally the same. No matter whether we are reaching for a glass of wine, signing up for a retirement plan, or heading to the gym after work, there's a moment at which our minds decide to initiate action. And that moment goes through a predictable script within the brain. You can think about that script as the CREATE funnel.[29]

The CREATE Funnel

In order for a person to take action, six things need to occur. Imagine an online retirement application that encourages people to review their contribution levels and allocations to make sure they are on track for a secure retirement. Most record keepers, like Vanguard, TIAA-CREF, and AON Hewitt, offer this functionality.

---

[29] This chapter, and the CREATE funnel in particular, build upon my book *Designing for Behavior Change,* published by O'Reilly Media, and a related Toolkit for practitioners that I developed at HelloWallet. This chapter applies the concepts from those two documents specifically to employee benefits.

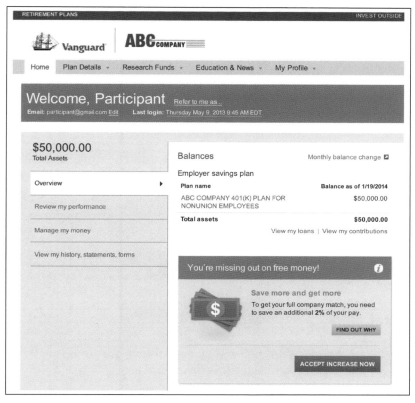

Figure 5: A common scenario — asking employees to change their
retirement contributions. *Image from Vanguard's retirement portal.*

Your employees already know that retirement planning is important,
and want to have a comfortable retirement. They also know that they
should keep abreast of changes in their accounts and financial
circumstances and plan accordingly. But how many employees
actually review their retirement contributions and allocations
regularly? Not many.[30]

A range of *practical and cognitive obstacles* can intervene to stop
someone from actually engaging with their benefits, even when they
want to. An understanding of these obstacles can help us move past

---

[30] For example, in 2012 only 12% of Vanguard's participants reallocated
existing balances (Vanguard 2013)

simply judging our employees (i.e., assuming they must be lazy or insincere) and toward effective solutions to help them take action.

We can see these obstacles in clearest relief at the moment of action (or the moment of failure to act). Plan design, incentives, and internal communications all come together to influence that specific moment of action. Behavioral researchers have found that when an individual takes action, six things occur:

- ❖ **Cue: Something cues the person to think about acting**. Why would your employees think about adjusting contributing levels? Maybe an email from HR or their retirement provider. Perhaps a discussion with friends, or a retirement ad on TV. Without a cue that gets them started, there's no way they will take action.

- ❖ **Reaction: The mind automatically reacts intuitively and emotionally.** What do your employees think about retirement? For many, it's a scary prospect they would rather avoid. With a strong negative reaction, you've lost the person — they won't take the action regardless of the benefits.

- ❖ **Evaluation. With conscious awareness, the mind does a quick cost-benefit analysis**. How hard it will be to do, what's the benefit, what are the other alternatives? For many employees, the value of *changing* contributions, once set, is unclear. They'll decide against it, and start thinking about something else.

- ❖ **Ability. The person must actually be able to act, and know it.** The person must know logistically what to do and have the resources and self-confidence to do it. If employees don't have their user name and password to the website, they can't change their retirement contribution even if they wanted to.

- ❖ **Timing. The person needs to have a reason to act now**, rather than doing something else that is more urgent. Employees may *want* to check on retirement contributions, but be busy doing something else.

- ❖ **Experience. The person takes action, and learns from that experience before deciding to act again.** By checking on retirement contributions, employees gain skills and confidence which can help them do it again. If they fail (perhaps because the site was too complex), they are *less* likely to try in the future. With each experience, employees adapt.

Together, they form the acronym CREATE since that is what's needed to CREATE action.

Leaks in the Funnel Mean Low Engagement with Benefits

You can think about these six stages as a leaky funnel, as shown in Figure 6, with two holes at each stage. On one side, employees may decide against signing up for a benefit because it's not valuable enough, it's not urgent, etc. On the other side, they may get distracted and do something else, like surfing the Internet. When employees face obstacles, they may be resolvable — but that process takes time and leaves the person open to further distraction.

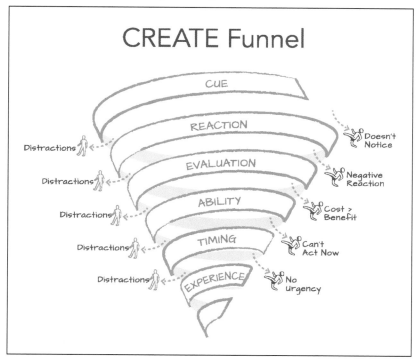

Figure 6: The CREATE funnel, 6 steps that occur if an employee takes action

For benefits that don't absolutely require a response from employees, you should start by *assuming* that people won't take action. It's not that employees are disinterested — it's the consequence of numerous small and large barriers represented by the CREATE funnel. On the way from inaction to action, these barriers will stop most of your employees, unless you work to remove them.

To make these obstacles concrete, think back to the example of an online program that encourages employees to adjust their retirement contributions. Imagine 100 long-time employees who have signed up for the company retirement plan, but haven't reviewed and adjusted their contribution levels in years. Your team sends them an email that reminds them to check their contribution levels. The majority of them, 70, see the email — that is, they detect your cue to act. The other 30 are on vacation with the kids, or swamped with other work, etc. By the time they look through their pile of email, they cursorily scan it for really important stuff and miss your email about retirement contributions.

Of those 70 who see the message, they first scan the subject line — "It's time to review your retirement contributions". The majority of them (50 out of 70) take you at your word, and open the email. The others have a quick gut reaction that makes them discard the message — some associate retirement with the distant future (not relevant now), some just scan the subject, see "retirement" and label it as something *they've already taken care of* (so it's not relevant now).

Of those that open and evaluate the content of the message, most (35) start reading and agree with the gist — thinking, yes, this is important to review. The others, a much smaller group (15) don't. Either they know that their contribution level is already fine, or they just don't see changing it as that important.

Of those who believe that reviewing their retirement contributions is important, most (24) actually remember their password to the retirement website. A smaller portion (11) doesn't, however, and has to search for it later or contact the HR department.

Finally, those who have their retirement password quickly look at the clock, and their dozens of other emails. Remarkably, most (17) think:

OK, I don't have anything more pressing. I'll do this now. And they execute the action — they log into the retirement site, review, and adjust their contributions.[31] The few others (7) have more pressing matters at hand.

Of those who take action, most (12) will be successful and can build on that experience in the future. A few (5) will get frustrated, however, and that negative experience will hinder them from making important contribution adjustments in the future

At each step of the way, roughly 70% of the employees were OK. A healthy majority: Honestly, one that is much larger than would actually occur in practice (70% of people think that adjusting retirement contributions in the middle of a work day is the most urgent of their time? Hardly!) Yet, only 17 people took action, and only 12 both took action and are likely to do so again in the future. The obstacles along the way are shown in Figure 7.

---

[31] In reality, employees could click on the email, but have problems on the site and fail to successfully complete the action. The CREATE funnel applies for each small action a person takes. But, this is just an example to show how easy it is for inaction to result in the *best* of circumstances.

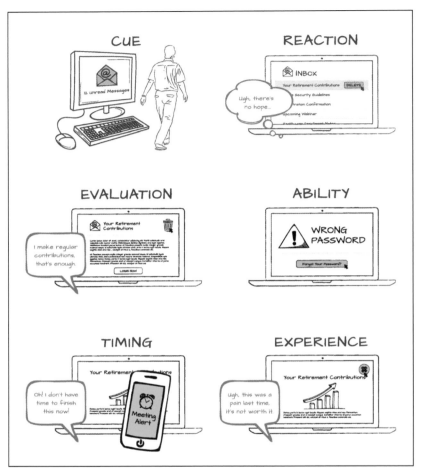

Figure 7: People often fail to adjust their retirement contributions,
stopping at each step of the way in the **CREATE** funnel

There's no magic here. There are reasonable, straightforward reasons that the vast majority of employees might not take action. Cumulatively, small barriers add up to a tremendously effective set of obstacles for employees. That's why it is vital to both identity the particular obstacles that employees face and use the tools of behavioral science to work around them.

With this understanding of how employees make benefits decisions as a foundation, let's look at some additional lessons that provide further depth and nuance.

There's Always Competition for Attention and Effort

An important lesson from the CREATE funnel, and the research behind it, is that employee decisions to act don't occur in a vacuum. Every possible action we could take is effectively in competition with every other action, at every moment in our lives. Anything could be cued. Anything might be urgent. Ironically, the onslaught of potential actions is made manageable by the simple limits of our minds — limited attention and mental resources to think about the range of options. The mind filters out all but a tiny fraction of the potential actions we could take, and focuses on the few that are relevant at the moment. Then, among the ideas that do come to mind (i.e., get cued), it's a battle for *relative* importance, *relative* urgency, *relative* ease of execution, etc.

What does this mean for employees and benefits decisions? It means that naturally and necessarily, employees aren't thinking about benefits all the time. And, they probably aren't thinking about their benefits much even when they "should" — around open enrollment time, when their family circumstances change, etc. — because benefits decisions are competing against a million other things that the employee could think about and do.

Because the competition for attention and effort is so fierce, we should be both realistic and forgiving when employees don't pay as much attention as they "should". Benefits decisions are important, but so are countless other things. It's our job, when designing and communicating benefits, to confront this challenge. We must sidestep or overcome the competing actions — just long enough that the employee can take the actions they need, and then get back to their lives.

Apply the Funnel for Each Employee Benefits Decision

Above, we used the example of an employee deciding whether or not to change his retirement contribution, and showed how the CREATE funnel works in that context. The same process occurs for every single sub-action employees might take around their benefits — deciding to open an email from HR, deciding to fill out and send in an election form based on that email, etc. For each sub-action, and each stage of the funnel within it, HR practitioners have a great deal of influence over whether employees succeed or fail.

For example, when we design and send an internal communication about benefits elections, we are subtly setting up the conditions for employees to take action or not. The communication itself serves as a *potential* cue — and the timing of the message, the subject line, and the sender all determine whether employees actually *detect* the cue. The subject line and high-level layout and content of the message shape the intuitive *reaction*, and the value proposition given in the email shape the *evaluation*.

Let's now examine each stage of the funnel, and what HR professionals can do to ensure that employees who want to take action aren't blocked.

A Deeper Look into Applying the CREATE Funnel

Consider a set of employees, all of whom are in a high-deductible healthcare plan, and are eligible for a health savings account (HSA). They haven't signed up for an HSA account yet, however, and thus haven't used one to put aside tax-sheltered money for future expenses. Most employees want to have money available when medical expenses arise. Most also want to save money on taxes, as HSAs can provide. But, we know that many employees are in exactly this situation — eligible for an HSA but not contributing.[32] How can HR professionals help employees go from inaction to action — to set up an HSA and start contributing?

---

[32] For example, see Dicken (2008), which shows that 49% of Americans in HSA-eligible plans at the time had not enrolled in an HSA; http://www.gao.gov/products/GAO-08-474R.

Cue

The cue to take action (setting up an HSA) can come in three forms:

❖ **Internal cues**. An employee may think about the action because of an internal process going on inside their heads. For example, their knee might start hurting, which leads them to start thinking about seeing the doctor, the money involved, the need to save up the money to pay for it, and, finally to setting up an HSA.

❖ **Existing external cues.** An employee may think about the action because of something in their daily environment — like an email from their doctor, a visit to a friend in the hospital, or a conversation with a spouse about the family budget.

❖ **New HR-related cues.** The HR team, or the company's vendors, might intentionally cue employees to think about action. For example: the HR team could hold an HSA sign-up event, or wellness ambassadors in the company might talk with their colleagues about the benefits of using the HSAs, or an HSA account provider like HSA Bank could send an email reminding people to enroll.

While only one of these types of cues is directly under the control of HR professionals, *all three* could trigger employees to think about action. If employees are already thinking about HDHPs and HSAs because of media coverage of the Affordable Care Act, then the HR team can move on to other obstacles that employees face. HR professionals don't need to do any cueing at all! Identifying where effort *isn't* needed is a key part of the process — so HR can find the gaps and focus their energies on filling them.

Sometimes, existing cues — both internal and external — occur regularly among certain segments of the population, and can be counted on to cue employees to think about action. People who are chronically ill are more likely to think about healthcare and medical expenses than those who aren't; the HR team can segment the population accordingly. For chronically ill people, HR might focus on later stages of the process (making it easy for employees to sign up, rather than trying to get them to think about medical issues in the first place). And, HR can better tailor communications to grab the attention of people who *aren't* chronically ill, and might need additional help to think about HSAs in the first place.

How well employees detect a cue depends on the channel used, and the employees' particular circumstances. For example, one employee group may check its corporate email very often, and be highly attentive to messages there. For others, corporate email is rarely paid attention to, but personal email is. There's unfortunately no hard and fast rule about what channel to use — there's an art to matching employee segments to appropriate communication channels.

The timing of cues is also important. First, it's important because you want to avoid competition. If you send an email at 9 a.m. on Monday, at a time when employees are sifting through hundreds of other emails, it's all too easy for your communication to get lost.

Second, timing is important because you want to cue people to act at a time when they are already thinking about similar things. The mind is more likely to detect a cue when it is primed to think about it. For example, during open enrollment people are generally thinking about benefits more (at least more than most other times of the year).[33] Again, there is no hard and fast rule about the timing of cues — but we'll get into the art of finding the right timing for your situation later on.

Reaction

Once employees are cued to think about HSA contributions, they will have an automatic and intuitive reaction. How would they react to the idea of using an HSA? For many employees, the simple idea of HSAs brings up negative emotions — not being able to pay the bills, having family members fall ill, etc. Conscious deliberation about HSAs as a tax-sheltered vehicle to *manage* these risks doesn't occur yet — the automatic emotional process starts before

---

[33] The exception is things that are highly novel or that are dangerous. Flying pigs get attention, no matter what. So do tigers running towards you. Unfortunately, animal cruelty laws prohibit their use by HR professionals in a systematic way; so, it's best to look for times when people are primed to think about benefits already.

deliberation. Unfortunately, such negative reactions can push the person to stop thinking about contributing to an HSA altogether.

To avoid this outcome — an automatic emotional rejection of an idea — it's useful to think about how those reactions occur. They are largely based on the prior experiences we've had, and the associations our minds have made between things. So, this means we need to understand a bit about our employees, and how they see the world.

If everything medical is associated with anxiety, then sidestep the association altogether. Present HSAs as tax savings, or as a budgeting tool (of course, there may be strong negative reactions there, too). By sidestepping the initial intuitive reaction, you can help individuals think *consciously* and *deliberatively* to determine whether they actually want to take action or not.

Automatic reactions extend not only to the *content,* but the *form* of messages that cue employees to act. Let's say that the HSA message comes within a larger benefits package (i.e., the *form* of the message). To be frank, many employees don't look forward to interacting with a thick benefits package at all. This emotional reaction can turn them away immediately, regardless of the content.

There are two strategies to use here: First, simply avoid the baggage. Avoid communications that look similar to what people dislike; it's better to break new ground and do something fresh than to try to overcome a negative association. Figure 8 has a nice example of an interactive benefits communications package known as ALEX that sidesteps employees' baggage around communications by making the application look (and act) differently.

A separate package isn't required though — at Rackspace, the HR team made its 401(k) information session look like "The Price Is Right" game show (with Phil White, then Director of Racker Rewards, as Bob Barker); they effectively sidestepped people's prior associations with boring retirement seminars, and had a bit of fun too.[34]

---

[34] Miller (2013); White (2014).

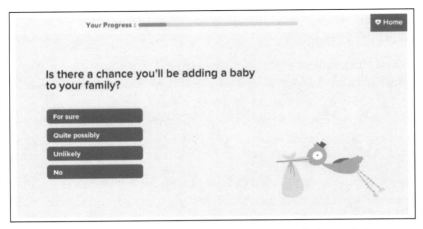

Figure 8: Jellyvision's ALEX avoids prior (and negative) associations
employees might have with benefits communications by
intentionally using a humorous, unique design.

Second, presentation matters. The message should look beautiful. Behavioral researchers have shown in painstaking detail how we really do judge a book by its cover.[35]

For many other employees, HSAs yield no automatic reaction at all, other than uncertainty. That's because many people simply don't know what they are and how they work. That blank slate is both an opportunity and a risk. It's an opportunity because of a lack of negatives — it's easier to step into a cognitive and deliberative process. It's a risk because things that are complex and unfamiliar evoke their own reactions.

Evaluation

HR professionals, like many other experts, are trained to appeal to someone's conscious evaluation of the costs and benefits of an action — like whether or not to use a benefit program. In our benefit communications, we know how to present the compelling

---

[35] See Gladwell (2005) for an easy to read analysis of our reactive judgments; see Wilson (2002) or Kahneman (2011) for a more scholarly treatment. Willis and Todorov (2006), for example, discuss how we judge people's faces in 1/10th of second.

value of a program. We show how the upside is great, and the downside is minor or can be avoided.

There are three key things to remember, however, about an employee's evaluation process.

First, motivation alone doesn't make a person act. It's certainly important to clearly express the benefits of taking action; but, that doesn't mean the other parts of the CREATE funnel (such as a cue to act and the intuitive reaction) can be ignored. Motivation is a *partial* substitute for other factors. With a strong motivation to act — e.g., knowing that one's child needed surgery — one can overcome logistical obstacles. But, it's often more direct to address the obstacle head-on.

Second, costs and benefits extend beyond money. It's not just the *financial incentives* a company offers that matter. As many HR professionals already know, social rewards — recognition by the company, and, especially, by one's friends, can be immensely powerful motivators. Chapter 5 discusses the role of financial and non-financial incentives in benefits implementation in greater detail.

Third, the evaluation is a personal and particular one. There are few universal motivators, and employees differ. An HSA, for example, can provide near- and long-term tax advantages. But, they are only relevant for those who have money to put away in the first place; if you don't have the money to pay for medical expenses at all, you also don't have the money to get the tax advantages of saving for them. So, like other areas of the CREATE funnel, designing benefits and communication around the conscious evaluation requires a thorough knowledge of the employee and his or her situation.

There are also significant limits on how employees consciously evaluate costs and benefits. First, there is the limitation of time — future benefits are weighted much less than present ones (even accounting for the present value of money). Behavioral economists call this "temporal myopia"; more informally, you can think of it as "I want it now". Retirement planning runs afoul of this limitation.

Another important limitation is our ability to accurately calculate the benefits of an action, which derives from many sources. Most people just aren't that good at making calculations in their heads. For example, we don't know how much our small, health-related items actually add up to each month (from contact lenses to co-pays). That makes it hard to calculate how much to contribute to an HSA and thus what the tax benefits would actually be.

We're also not financially literate, by and large. For example, it's difficult for most people (including myself!) to fully grasp the true power of compound interest of retirement savings.[36] Or, how much money we're losing by only paying the minimums on our credit cards. Finally, our minds rarely handle expected returns as the mathematically correct sum of probabilities times value. We overestimate the importance of vivid risks, and underestimate other infrequent risks. We fear loss twice as much as we value a similar gain.[37]

How can an HR professional support action amid this morass of limitations and cognitive biases? One way is to skip them altogether — and do the necessary calculations for people. Instead of singing the praises of HSA-tax advantages, offer a concrete amount that the person might save in taxes; dollar figures are readily comparable. Instead of highlighting the long-term importance of retirement savings, find ways to decrease the near-term costs (easy enrollment, defaulting, etc.).

Ability

Assuming employees have the desire to act, they must have the ability to take action as well. You can think about the ability to act in terms of three dimensions:

❖ **Resources**. Does the employee have the necessary time, money, or skills to act? For an employee who wants to sign up for an HSA, does she realistically have money to spare? If sign-up is only through an online HR portal, does she have access to the site and does it support her browser or mobile phone?

---

[36] See McKenzie and Liersch (2011).

[37] See Kahneman and Tversky (1984), Tversky and Kahneman (1973).

❖ **Logistics**. Does the employee know *how* to take action? I.e., where to sign up for the HSA and how to make a contribution?

❖ **Confidence**. Does the employee think he will actually be able to take the action? People are much less likely to *try* to do something if they think they will fail — they have better things to do with their time.

Along each dimension, HR professionals can remove obstacles to help employees act: by providing resources or the limiting need for them, giving clear logistical information, and reframing the task as one that employees are confident they can undertake.

This starts by clearly identifying those obstacles: Are employees blocked from using the benefits providers' website at work because of a firewall? Is the clinic used in the wellness program too far from the office and employees' homes? Or, are employees getting to the retirement website but can't figure out how to actually change their elections?

Simplifying the task itself that employees are asked to undertake can have tremendous impact on each aspect of employee ability. For example, researchers have found that decreasing the number of options in a retirement plan from dozens to a few well-diversified options can increase the likelihood that employees will choose *something* — employees need less time (resources) to make a choice, and they can be more confident that they can found a reasonably good option.

Timing

Many benefits decisions are "always important but never urgent." Exercising with a wellness program is great — but one could always start exercising tomorrow. Retirement is clearly vital, but it's often many years away, and there's always time to catch up (until it's too late, of course). Medical expenses are important, but you can always contribute to an HSA later.

In the face of that lack of inherent urgency, the benefits world *creates* urgency during open enrollment periods.[38] Employees will sign up for retirement (or not) during a specific period because they can't postpone it — they have to make a choice for the year. The limited duration of open-enrollment places additional weight on the decision and makes the person more likely to take *some type* of action.[39]

One challenge with this approach to urgency, however, is: What happens after the period is over, and follow-up actions are required? *Signing up* for a wellness program is nice; actually going to the gym or a stress reduction class is much more important. And so, it still falls to the HR professional and vendors to find ways to ensure appropriate urgency for *each* action the employee wants to take.

How else can an HR team create a sense of urgency? One way is to create *events* — HSA enrollment sessions, wellness classes, and retirement workshops. An expert or trainer might come to the jobsite on a specific day — forcing the issue of taking action or not. Another is to create or promote news: something that will quickly lose relevance, and that the person actually values. Look for information that is intrinsically interesting to employees and loses immediacy rapidly. For example: Updates from friends who are trying to meet their fitness goals; that's something that exercise trackers, like FitBit, do well.[40] "The Biggest Loser" and other workplace competitions also create time pressure to act, in which there is ongoing feedback between competitors that spurs them to push forward.

Each of these approaches to *creating* a sense of urgency around employee action has its downsides. The most obvious downside is that making a program available for a limited period of time means some people can't participate if their schedules or circumstances don't align with that timing. Sending out an email offering incentives

---

[38] I haven't seen a scientific study of employee benefits uptake with and without open enrollment, but it would be fascinating to test whether, and how much, the open enrollment period affects sign-up.

[39] Which may entail deciding against retirement contributions, of course.

[40] Some HR departments try this with newsletters, but they may lack the inherent interest of their intended readers.

to people who act in the next five minutes falls flat on employees who are away from email for the next half hour.

Another downside from creating urgency for each action an employee should take is that it becomes shrill over time. "Limited time offer … Limited time offer … Limited time offer …" we've all seen that in retail ads. We just don't get the same reaction over time if it is too sensational. The loss of power, ironically, can be mitigated by not unduly stressing the urgency. Open enrollment is an example of this: That's just the policy. It's not a gimmick, it's just how it is. There are *urgent reminders* about the limited nature of open enrollment, but HR doesn't develop new, catchier open-enrollment periods each time (this year you only have two minutes for open enrollment instead of two weeks!).

Experience

If each of the five preceding stages go smoothly (cue-reaction-evaluation-ability-timing) then the person can execute the action. As noted above, the act of taking action, or failing to act, changes the equation the next time around: the person has gained experience.

Using our HSA enrollment example, let's say the employee sees the value of signing up. The employer sends out an email cueing them to act, and saying that it's important to act soon, so as not to miss out on the tax savings. Well, what if the employee *doesn't* act? Maybe she got distracted while looking for the HSA website and forgot. A month later, her HR department sends her *another* email about signing up for HSAs. This time around, things are different. Clearly, failing to sign up for the HSA last time wasn't the end of the world. The employee's *perceived* urgency to act decreases. Moreover, after *multiple* reminders, they start to fade into the background; they lose their power to cue the person to act.[41]

You can think of the effect of an action *now* on action *in the future* in terms of how it affects:

❖ The person's skills, expertise, and knowledge.

---

[41] HelloWallet has done research on this topic with email reminders

❖ The person's beliefs about what's normal.

Skills and expertise generally *build* over time with experience. If the person takes action, she gains skills and expertise that make it more likely to take action in the future. If she *does not* take action, there's no effect on skills and expertise. Knowledge is more complex. If the person took action and had a positive experience, concrete knowledge of the benefits of action can increase the likelihood that the person will act in the future. Concrete knowledge that the action is difficult or not rewarding makes it far less likely — it's very difficult to win back someone who knows first-hand that they don't like the action. If the person doesn't take action, her knowledge about the urgency of the action may change, as described above, but otherwise her overall knowledge doesn't change.

A person's beliefs about normal behavior also change because of experiences, and what she sees from her friends. Internally, we're largely what social psychologist Tim Wilson calls "strangers to ourselves"[42] — we don't really know what we might do until we actually do it. So, when we take an action, we naturally see ourselves as someone who takes that action normally[43] — we use the experience to inform our understanding of who we are, and what we should do in the future. Action begets action. Similarly, we're constantly watching our friends and colleagues to see what's "normal" to do when we're unsure; if we see them taking action, we're more likely to act in the future, and vice-versa.

Summary

The six stages, cue-reaction-evaluation-ability-timing-experience, form the CREATE funnel. Each stage contains potential obstacles that may confront employees. At each step along the way, employees naturally and necessarily get distracted or decide to do something else; thus, we can visualize the funnel as having multiple leaks.

---

[42] See Wilson (2002)'s book by that title.

[43] That's assuming that the experience doesn't go horribly awry, and we realize we made a mistake and the action doesn't fit our self-conception.

The CREATE funnel is a tool you can use to identify what, exactly, is hindering your employees' action — why they aren't crossing the gap between intention and action. It's a checklist for programs, yours or someone else's. When designing and implementing benefits packages, the goal is to find and plug the leaks.

Habits

There's another, potentially profound way in which employee behavior changes over time: forming and changing habits.

Habits are created when a behavior is frequently repeated after a consistent cue.[44] Habits are the mind's way of outsourcing control over behavior to the environment, as leading habit researcher Wendy Wood describes. The brain learns to automatically execute a behavior whenever the cue occurs. For example, when I see my gym clothes on Saturday morning, I get ready to go to the gym.

Habits are essential because they free our minds to think about other things. That's why we can drive to work, and think about what we're going to do at the office, at the same time.[45]

From an HR and benefits perspective, habits help employees lock in new behaviors: whether they be exercising regularly or checking a budget. Unfortunately, they take a long time to form — anywhere from a few weeks to months, depending on the person and situation.[46] The employer can't really form a habit for employees though; it can only set up the environment in which the employee

---

[44] See Wood and Neal (2007) for more information on this process. See Dean (2013) for a recent summary of the research on habits.

[45] It's not because we "multitask" by thinking about multiple things at once — we can't really do that (e.g., Hamilton 2008). Our conscious minds give attention to one thing at a time. It's because our minds just aren't "thinking" about driving at all — they are relying on learned patterns of behavior and capture conscious attention only when needed, like when facing a novel or dangerous situation (a detour or an imminent car crash).

[46] See Lally et al. (2010). Research on how and under what conditions habits form is just getting started. See Clear (2014) on the myth of 21-day habits.

may choose to repeat an action again and again, until a habit forms. For that, we can use the CREATE funnel.

A Quick Recap

❖ For an employee to take action on her benefits, six things need to occur — a cue that starts her thinking about the action, an emotional reaction that pulls her forward or pushes her away, a more careful evaluation of costs and benefits, an assessment of the ability to act, as assessment of the right timing for action, and, if executed, the experience changes her skills, knowledge, and beliefs.

❖ At each stage, employees get distracted or get blocked against further action. In order for programs to be most effective, find the obstacles and distractions and remove them.

❖ Because so many factors need to come together at once for employees to take action on their benefits, and they have so many *competing* actions they could take, we shouldn't be surprised when employees fail to act. Instead, we should systematically identify competing factors and sidestep or overcome them when doing so helps employees act in their own interests.

❖ Habits are born of repetition — doing the same action again and again in response to a cue. They can allow employees to lock in a new behavior (like exercise) in the long-term, but require the same CREATE process when the employee is just starting out.

3
THE 6-STEP BENEFITS PROCESS, INTEGRATING BEHAVIORAL RESEARCH

This chapter is about how you and your team can leverage behavioral techniques at each stage of the benefits process.

In Chapter 2, the CREATE funnel provided a framework for thinking about the quirks of the mind, and the behavioral obstacles they cause. Later on, we'll show how these obstacles can be overcome with techniques like auto-enrollment, social competitions, and other, more exotic techniques like loss aversion and priming effects. These techniques are intriguing to think about, exciting to explore in practice, and impressive to tell your colleagues about.

However, they are only half of the behavioral story. Those techniques are the *outcomes* of behavioral research; behavioral *methods* also can inform each stage of plan design and delivery. In this chapter, we'll give a quick overview of a behaviorally informed benefits process: The ACTION model. Most of the rest of the book, in fact, is structured around the ACTION model and provides additional detail and guidance.

The ACTION Model

Each year, HR practitioners review their current programs and priorities, and their available budget, to plan out which broad changes to make, which vendors to use (if any), how to structure the revised programs, how to deploy them to employees, and how to evaluate their impact.[47] A behavioral approach can provide value and insight at each stage of this process — augmenting the existing expertise of HR practitioners.

In particular, it can provide insight into how the HR team Analyzes employee needs; how it Crafts changes to benefits offerings, or *benefits interventions*; how they Test early concepts and refine them; how the Implement the intervention in full, and how they Observe the behavioral impact; and how the team plans to Navigate the lessons learned and shifting priorities that arise as the next benefits cycle begins.

We first looked at this spiral of benefits ACTION in Chapter 1, in which each iteration brings the benefits offerings closer in line with the needs of the workforce and company. Here, we'll introduce the lessons behavioral research has to offer in each stage of the process. This chapter provides an overview for senior managers; subsequent chapters return to many of these topics and provide tactical tips for practitioners in the field.

---

[47] These actions are often divided into three broad phases (which go by many names): Design, Implementation, and Evaluation.

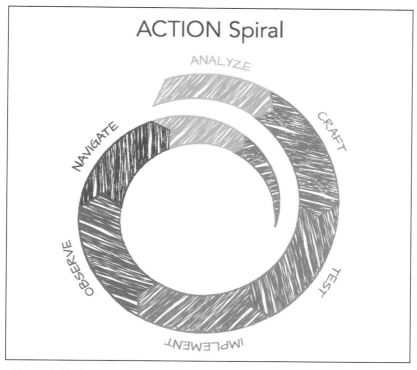

Figure 9: Six Steps for Integrating Behavioral Science into Employee Benefits

An Example: Wellness at Company X

To better understand how behavioral methods can be applied to benefits, we'll need a concrete example to work with. Let's use a common scenario: A company choosing among potential wellness programs. It's a scenario that captures some of the changing dynamics of the benefits space, and the enduring issues that always confront HR professionals as they examine their benefits offerings.

A Normal Benefits Selection Process

Consider Company X, a nationwide retail company with a diverse workforce: a range of salespeople, supporting office staff, and managers. X's workforce has slowly become more sedentary and unhealthy over time. X saw it in its medical bills, worker productivity, and in the simple human factors visible all around the office — expanding waistlines, poor diet, and low energy. Even the younger members were increasingly prone to diabetes and its many negative consequences. (Unfortunately, this is a very common scenario.)

Faced with an increasingly unhealthy workforce, X's HR department decided to investigate wellness programs. Jackie was tasked with evaluating what was out there and picking the best option for Company X.

She searched the Internet and talked with her broker, and one particular program seemed like a promising add-on to traditional wellness programs — a weight loss competition, much like "The Biggest Loser" TV show. Jackie had seen "The Biggest Loser" on TV and talked about the show with other employees at X before. It was straightforward, something the company could rally around, and everyone had seen its success on TV. She chose it, and her boss signed off on it.

Over the next few months, she worked with the vendor to fine-tune the program, and developed internal communications to the staff. After a few pre-events in X stores to build awareness and excitement, they launched the program.

And, the employees loved it! Company X signed up 60 teams. There was a big party to launch it, and there was a lot of chatter in the company about the competition. Collectively, the teams lost more than 3,000 pounds. A ton and a half of weight. There was another big event to mark the end of the competition and to celebrate the winners.

But 60 teams weren't anywhere close to the entire staff of the company. Only one-third of the employees who really needed it actually joined the program. Among those who did, some weren't really trying after a few weeks. Even the top teams seemed to regain the weight a few weeks or months after the competition ended.

Some members of the HR team could look to the success stories — the people who lost weight, the joy in team members' eyes as they cheered each other on. Other members looked at the low follow through, and the high cost of incentives for the program, and wondered whether it was really worth it.

Over the course of the year, the CFO's office didn't see any clear change in healthcare costs, especially given all of the other changes going on at the same time in health care. The Chief Human Resources Officer tried to tell a compelling story to the rest of senior management, but the facts were clearly mixed.

Was this a good use of company resources and employee time?

The honest answer is that we probably don't know. At least, not yet.

The Behavioral Approach

How might a behavioral researcher assess the success or failure of a wellness program like this? At a high level, the behavioral approach doesn't suggest anything different than what HR professionals already do: Analyze needs, develop programs, and determine their impact. But let's look at the details.

Analyze. The first step would be to analyze what's needed, starting with a clear definition of the outcome that the company seeks. For example:

> *Target Outcome: Lower the incidence of diabetes and pre-diabetes cases by 10%.*

That goal may translate into a specific bottom-line impact that the company's CFO seeks in terms of bending the healthcare cost curve. Perhaps it's not cost-oriented, though; the program's sole motivation may come from of a basic concern for the long-term welfare of employees.

As part of the diagnosis process, a researcher would want to better understand the employee population and what's preventing them from achieving the outcome (avoiding diabetes) on their own. Do the employees want to achieve the outcome themselves? Do they have sufficient motivation to do so? If they do have motivation, do they a lack a sense of urgency, or resources (time, money) to live differently? Identifying that specific obstacle helps tailor the intervention, using the CREATE model.

For example:

> *Primary obstacles for employees: Timing and Ability (the "T" and "A" in CREATE). Employees feel no sense of urgency, and have few practical resources to prevent diabetes in the near term.*

It also helps to consider whether the company's goal is a long-term one that won't be measurable quickly, or a near-term goal. Our example, decreasing the incidence of diabetes, is a lofty one, and thus the company should also set earlier sub-goals against which they can measure progress.

Craft. Next, one would design the benefits intervention — evaluating potential changes to benefits offerings based on what the company really cares about. The team would analyze the concrete actions employees might take that will help them overcome *or sidestep* the CREATE obstacles. What's likely to decrease diabetes among these particular employees? Which would help the most: Losing weight, healthier eating, or more exercise? For example:

> *Primary intervention: avoid the need for urgency by affecting habitual eating (aka "Mindless Eating").[48] Help employees eat healthier by adding fiber rich ingredients and whole grains.*

If a new program is required, the team would analyze the information provided by vendors or consultants, and assess the quality of that evidence. The team would also fine-tune the program to the particular needs of their employees.

Test. *As the intervention is being crafted,* find rapid cost-effective ways to test the idea before it is fully baked into a formal program. For many companies, that means a pilot program with a subset of their employees or locations. Ideally however, a test can occur on a much smaller, and more cost-effective scale; the goal is to find problems early, before they become expensive. In the software world, this part of what's known as the "Lean Startup" approach.[49]

---

[48] See Wansink (2010)

[49] Following Eric Ries's (2011) book, *The Lean Startup.*

The team should focus its attention on testing the aspects of an intervention that seem most risky. For example, instead of launching a formal program to have employees change their plate sizes at home and at work, a simpler, more Lean approach would be this:

> *Risk identified in proposed intervention: Will employees consciously decide to continue to eat unhealthy meals at the cafeteria?*
>
> *Early testing: One morning, move fiber-rich foods closer in the cafeteria line and make unhealthier options less convenient. See how employees react.*

Each test will be imperfect, and incomplete. But by running small simple tests, the HR team can gather vital information about employees and where programs are likely to go awry.

Implement. The team then implements the program with awareness-raising activities, internal communications, administrative details, etc. Here's where a behavioral researcher would employ the well-known "tricks of the trade" — such as careful framing of messages to encourage action, intelligent defaults, competitions, expert and colleague-level endorsements, etc. For example:

> *Techniques used during intervention: changing ease of use and friction for various options (choice architecture), perhaps also with peer comparisons.*

These techniques help ensure that each aspect of the CREATE funnel is in place — that employees are cued to think about the program, understand its relevant costs and benefits, know they have the ability to succeed, etc.

Observe. After time, one would naturally want to *observe* the program in action and evaluate it. For a behavioral researcher, the key question for evaluation isn't *what did people do*, but rather, *what did they did do differently than they would have done otherwise?* In the Company X example: Were the people who were most engaged in the program, and lost the most weight, simply the sample people who would have done it anyway? And there's a related question: How do the cost and impact of the program compare to other possible interventions the company could have deployed?

To answer these questions, behavioral researchers have a particular tool which is the gold standard for cutting through the noise and understanding the real impact of a program: the randomized control trial. Employees would be randomly assigned to receive different versions of the intervention (or no intervention at all), and their outcomes would be compared afterwards. For example:

> *Means to evaluate intervention: Randomly select a subset of employees to be initially invited for a special company lunch program, where the healthier options have been moved closer; over time, invite all other employees (i.e., a "staggered rollout" experimental design).*

The goal we initially set, reducing the incidence of diabetes and pre-diabetes was a lofty one, and one that will likely take quite a bit of time.

Navigate. For many behavioral researchers, the next step would be to confront the imperfections and refine over time. Such as, the researcher would expect, from the beginning of the process, to be at least partially wrong. To need to make adjustments. To learn as you go.

Nothing works exactly as planned, especially when it comes to trying to change behavior; even with early testing, the vagaries of human behavior mean we're always surprised in the end. And so, the team would plan on iteratively navigating the process and course correcting as needed.

> *Potential refinements: Give the healthy options new names, to demonstrate the artisanal nature of their sourcing and preparation,[50] and overcome prior associations employees have with "healthy = boring".*

---

[50] See Wansink (2010).

The Details Matter

At a high level the process — analyze, craft, test, implement, observe, navigate — is quite ordinary. It's basically what Jackie did too, at a high level. The difference lies in the details — in additional considerations and tools that a behavioral researcher would add that complement the existing expertise of HR professionals.

For Company X, the process could have been improved, especially when crafting the program by understanding whether a "Biggest Loser" competition was, in fact the best way to improve the health of the workforce in the long run (research studies have shown that high-pressure, short-term diet programs in fact are ineffective, or even detrimental in the long run).[51]

> *The cheapest solutions, in terms of time and money, are the ones employed early in the process before a benefit program is fully implemented and its problems become painfully obvious.*

Jackie also could have used tools from the behavioral sciences to cut through vendor claims and better assess what the likely impact on her particular workers would be (case studies can be incredibly powerful, and misleading, unfortunately).

The process at Company X also could be improved during the observation phase. No one wants a scenario in which the evidence is mixed, people accuse each other of mistakes and misrepresentations, and there's no clear way to say who is right and who is wrong other than force of argument. Tools from the behavioral sciences, such as spin-free data analyses and randomized control trials, can help ensure that at the end of a pilot or program implementation everyone can be on the same page and clear about what to do next.

---

[51] See for example, Haupt (2010), Pappas (2010), Wilson and Hayes (2014) for an introduction to some of the issues with Biggest Loser and other rapid weight loss-approaches.

Thus in the Company X case, the Craft and Observe phases appeared to need the most attention. For other companies and scenarios, however, the need might be elsewhere. Applying a behavioral approach to benefits doesn't mean dictating what HR professionals should do — instead it provides tools to help them do what they do better.

The following chapters of the book dig into these processes in more detail. We'll start with an understanding of how employees make decisions about benefits, and then walk through each step in developing and deploying benefits interventions.

A Quick Recap

❖ Too often, after a benefit program is implemented, disagreements arise about whether or not the program is successful — because the goals were not clearly outlined in the beginning, and the outcomes were not rigorously tested along the way.

❖ HR practitioners can integrate behavioral lessons, especially a focus on employee behavior and outcomes, at each stage of a benefits development, from analyzing needs, crafting, testing, and implementing the new benefit program, observing it in practice and navigating the challenges that inevitably arise. These six stages can be remembered with the mnemonic ACTION.

❖ One of the tenets of ACTION is that teams should analyze a range of benefits interventions before deciding on the "obvious" way to improve outcomes. For example, instead of running a weight-loss competition, a much less expensive (and longer lasting) solution might be changing the physical design of company cafeterias and vending machines.

SECTION 2:
BENEFITS & BEHAVIORAL
RESEARCH IN PRACTICE

4
ANALYZING THE NEED

Benefit programs are subject to change: from new government requirements, to evolving employee needs, to changing costs to the company, HR has to adapt. In this chapter, we'll start to systematically look at these changes, and how employers can ensure they are responding appropriately — based on how employees are likely to actually react and use their benefits.

It's a four-step process.

1. **Clarifying the company's goals**. Example: The company wants to decrease healthcare costs.

2. **Defining the range actions that employees *might* take** that meet those goals. Example: exercising more, smoking less, paying more for healthcare.

3. **Understanding employee desires and needs**, especially whether employees actually want to take action. Example: Employees will strongly resist efforts to make them pay more for health care, but want help to become healthier and exercise more.

4. **Identify the right benefits intervention** that matches employee desires and employer goals.

In this chapter, we'll cover steps 1-3; step 4 is a large topic on its own, and is covered in the next chapter.

Make Sure the Company's Goals Are Clear

37% Higher Sales

43% More Productivity

50% Less Safety Incidents

125% Lower Burnout (sic)

300% More Innovation

These numbers come from a single infographic for the wellness program Virgin Pulse, labeled on its website as "Why Virgin".[52] To be fair to Virgin, it listed stats about employee happiness,[53] and made a case that Virgin Pulse improves happiness and employee engagement, which then solved a long list of corporate problems such as these. And, with a quick look at many other wellness providers, you'll encounter similar stats about broad and diverse impacts of their programs.

It's easy to be dazzled by the varied ROIs that benefit programs can offer. Unfortunately, it's often not clear exactly what these numbers mean and when they can (or can't) be trusted. Disentangling the claims, and determining what programs will really benefit employees and their employer, we should start with a simple question: *What's the real goal of a benefit program?*

Since these numbers come from a wellness program, let's specifically ask: Why would an HR department buy any wellness program at all? To boost productivity? To decrease health costs? To make employees feel appreciated by their company and retain them?

---

[52] Accessed at http://us.virginhealthmiles.com/fresh_approach/Pages/FreshApproach.as px 1 August 2013. The infographic with those numbers is no long available on their site. But yes, it did claim to offer a more than 100% decrease in burnout.

[53] Originally from http://deliveringhappinessatwork.com/why-it-matters/. Virgin cites the article by FastCompany http://www.fastcompany.com/3009940/dialed/happiness-secrets-from-the-staff-of-delivering-happiness-at-work which reprinted them.

If your team can't answer that question, clearly and succinctly, there's potentially serious trouble up ahead. Here are a few reasons why:

❖ **Impossible, unstated, expectations**. Unclear goals may mean someone in senior management is going to be upset at the outcomes. Perhaps you're designing a wellness program to decrease turnover, but members of the leadership team aren't on the same page and see it is a tool to decrease costs. It if retains employees, but does so by *slightly increasing* costs, your team will be attacked for doing the wrong job well.

❖ **Misaligned programs.** It's easy for vendors to get people excited about the *possible* benefits of a program, and for companies to say "Yes, I want that!" (Sure, we all want a 300% increase in innovation, whatever that means). But, that may or may not be what employees actually want and need. Clear goals help HR teams turn around the conversation — talking with employees first, then vendors, to identify programs that meet the expressed needs of employees.

❖ **No way to hold vendors accountable**. Unclear goals mean that it will be difficult to measure whether they are actually met. The evaluation of a benefit program then becomes an exercise in spin and counter-spin with your vendor (or with an internal team if it is implementing the program), when it should be a straightforward analysis of the facts.

❖ **No proof of success internally.** Without solid numbers to back up the program, it becomes difficult to defend successful, valuable programs against budget cuts and disagreements within the company.

The idea of having clear goals for benefit programs isn't new. But from a behavioral perspective, the need is magnified when we're looking at changes in human behavior. No single wellness program can deliver on all of the promises listed above (innovation, sales, presenteeism, etc.); there are always trade-offs. Instead, some programs will be good at some things, and not others; so in order to find the right one, you have to know what you're looking for.

Look for the Specific Outcomes

As you think about the goal of a program from a behavioral perspective, ask: What is the final, most meaningful outcome that the company seeks? Often, this analysis starts with a problem. For example: The company is losing valuable job candidates because they think the retirement benefits are stingy, or older workers aren't retiring on time and that's driving up the average healthcare costs for the company.

Let's imagine that the company wants to improve its retirement benefits. What does it mean to improve benefits, exactly? From a behavioral perspective, there are three parts to that question: the concrete, measurable thing that the company wants (*the outcome*), the behavior someone needs to take to improve that outcome (*the behavior*), and how well that behavior actually drives the desired outcome (*the impact*).

Retirement benefits provide a great example of the diverse outcomes that a company might seek. A company may want to improve the acceptance rate of its job offers. Or it may want to decrease the total cost of retirement expenses without increasing turnover. Or it may need to pass federal non-discrimination tests for the 401(k) plan.

It doesn't matter what the outcome is, as long as it's clear. For the sake of example, let's say that a company is interested in the long-term retirement readiness of their employees, and the outcome they care about is having more money in employee retirement accounts.

The outcome should be the final deliverable, not something that might to be a proxy for it. In the retirement space, people often use financial literacy events and retirement planning seminars to encourage employees to increase their contributions. Then, they measure employee engagement, participation, or financial literacy to show the impact of program. Is that what companies really want to know about their retirement program? Probably not.

You can think the final outcome like this: If X happened, and nothing else, would you consider the program a success? If employees participated in a retirement planning workshop, but they didn't actually increase their retirement contributions, would the program be a success? No. And, in reverse, if the program led to increased retirement contributions, but no one cared about the planning workshop, would it be a success? Probably yes.

The outcome must be measurable. Another way of thinking about the target is this: Will it be possible to say that the program clearly and definitively *failed*?[54] Is there a threshold by which a third party could evaluate the program and call it a failure from the company's perspective? That question makes it hard to use vague goals like "employee education," and focuses attention on things that are measurable. For example, a company may decide that anything less than an average 2% increase in employee contributions to their retirement plan is a failure.

Set sub-goals that are measurable quickly: leading indicators. If the goal that the company seeks is a long-term lofty one, then there's a problem. Sure, maybe the company wants to improve the retirement readiness of its employees, but that isn't going to change for months or even years. In this case, they should set specific and measurable sub-goals. Those sub-goals follow the same rules as the goal itself — if the sub-goal doesn't occur, is the program a failure? Make it something measurable in the real world, rather than an attitude in someone's head?

Another way of thinking of the sub-goal is as a "leading indicator" — something that we are reasonably certain precedes and predicts our final outcome. Employees increasing their retirement contributions is a leading indicator of improved retirement readiness. Attending a retirement seminar is not. When employees eat consistently healthier food, that is a leading indicator of decreased diabetes rates; *promising* to eat healthier is not.

The target outcome need not be simplistic. The company's target outcome may entail multiple sub-goals, any of which (or all of which) must be met for the program to succeed. It can tie together the diverse goals

---

[54] Usually success is easy to claim; preparing to accept failure motivates harder questions; don't worry — the whole point of this exercise is so that the program *won't* fail.

of the company, as long as they're clear and measurable. For example, the company wants employees to increase their net contributions by 2% OR increase the portion of job candidates that accept their offers by 10%. If the company leadership can agree to that, it's a good outcome that can support behavioral plan design.

Identify the Target Employees

After identifying the target outcome (like a 2% increase in retirement contributions), the next step is to ask *who* the company most wants to impact with the benefit program. Even if a program will be offered to all employees (for legal, policy, practical, or other reasons), companies can still think carefully about who *needs* a program the most, and who should be especially supported to take action. For a wellness program, for example, are you seeking to attract young healthy people, or improve the health of a sedentary segment of your existing employee base?

The reason *why* the company would target a particular segment for improved outcomes isn't relevant here. The behavioral approach to benefits doesn't try to dictate company policy or goals. It does, however, state that your company and HR team should be clear on who, exactly, you're trying to work with.

Define the Actions Employees *Might* Take

It may seem obvious, but the next step is to clearly specify what employees might *potentially* do that aligns with these goals — i.e. what will make the target outcome happen. For example, if the company seeks to increase the retirement readiness of its employees then the obvious focus should be helping employees increase their retirement contributions, right? Not necessarily.

An employee's retirement readiness is a product of many things — including the contribution rate, the asset allocation, the match formula, and the withdrawal rate. The contribution rate and withdrawal rate are driven by non-retirement behaviors like the overall debt to income ratio of the individual, and the individual's total savings rate. Low non-retirement savings rates and high debts drive withdrawals. One way to increase retirement balances is to ensure that people can afford to contribute to retirement and keep the money in the plan even when emergency expenses arise. Another way is to increase the company's match formula (though at a significant financial cost). *The most effective route may not be the obvious one.*

So, the next step is to force yourself and the team to look beyond the obvious, and come up with non-obvious ways that your employees could succeed. List them out as potential options. Remember, we're not looking for what they *will* do (not yet) — just what they *might* do.

Let's illustrate this step with the example we explored above: Say you're looking to decrease healthcare costs without alienating your employees. What possible actions could employees take that would decrease company healthcare costs? Perhaps:

❖ Exercising more

❖ Eating healthier foods

❖ Regularly taking maintenance drugs for chronic conditions

❖ Accepting an increase in their healthcare premiums[55]

❖ Switching to a healthcare plan that costs the employer, and hopefully the employee, less money

❖ Using a HSA (and saving both the employer and employee on taxes)

There's quite a range of approaches that one could take to decrease healthcare costs; some will be better than others. We're trying to generate a list; we're not ready to critique it yet.

---

[55] Note that this is the action the employee might take. Normally, we would think of healthcare premiums as a product of the insurance market and the costs employers pass on to their employees. Here though, we want to keep laser focused on employees — what they do. They always have a choice — even if that choice means quitting the company.

We are specifically looking for creative, new ideas. One way to do this is to think about obstacles. For example, why don't employees use hospital services less, or sign up for an HSA account? What's needed to overcome those obstacles? Do employees need greater confidence that they will be able to afford their basic expenses? Would incentives to use urgent care instead of hospitals overcome that obstacle? We're not looking for the answer itself — we're looking to generate new ideas for actions that employees might take.

Another approach is to use random words and see what ideas they trigger. Edward De Bono, the man who coined the term "Lateral Thinking", advocated this method.[56] It's another way to force ourselves to go beyond the obvious.

You'll also notice that these ideas aren't necessarily about specific programs to purchase. That's because at this point, we're intentionally not thinking about benefit programs *per se*. We are focusing on employee behaviors because that's where the rubber hits the road — either employees use the benefit or not. And now that we have a set of potential actions, some of which are unconventional or even unrealistic, let's look at the employee's needs and desires, and where company and employee needs align.

Get to Know Your Employees

Gather What You Know

Given the list of things that employees *might* do, let's gather what you know about employees and what they are likely to actually do.

If you have an existing program in place that you are unsatisfied with, like a wellness program, ask: What's the participation rate? How long do people stay engaged? What's the chatter around the office about the program? You probably already have a good sense of that.

---

[56] See De Bono (1973)

If there isn't a program already in place, you'll still already have a good base of knowledge on which to build — how often have people expressed a desire for this type of program? Are there similar programs that have been tried in the past but discontinued, and is there institutional knowledge about them?

Assess Desire

We want to know, for each of the possible actions and benefits above, whether employees would actually like them and use them?

The problem is: We can't really ask them. At least, not directly.

In the consumer products space, researchers have long since learned that if you ask someone what they like, it can have little to no relationship to what they actually "feel" or will do in the future:

❖ What happens when you ask employees whether they like an existing program or benefits campaign? The response says a lot about who they are, and how they feel about you. It doesn't tell you clearly how they feel about the product itself. If they like you, they'll likely say yes. If they're generally positive and optimistic, they'll likely say yes. If they want you to go away, they'll say whatever they think will do the trick. Their actual future behavior is very difficult to know.[57]

❖ What happens if you ask people whether they *want* a new program? Not surprisingly, the answer is general yes — as long as the employee isn't required to pay for it because they said so. We all want the *option* to use a benefit; unless it is absolutely terrible, we're happier to have the option than not have the option. That's the safe answer. Unfortunately, if an employer goes through all the hassle and expense of

---

[57] See Chapter 6 for some of the problems with self-reports on surveys. Honestly, we don't know ourselves. The conscious deliberative process that we may use to answer survey questions isn't the same part of the brain that may decide whether or not to engage with a wellness program or other benefit; it's only part of the picture.

providing the option of using a benefit for employees and no one actually uses it (or sets up a benefits fair the people don't attend, etc.), that's a colossal waste of time and money.

So, what can you do? Ideally, *observe instead of asking,* like with a sample election form. The challenge is that they need to take it seriously — it can't be a fake scenario, so there should be some form of *cost* of the choice.

> *Give employees a sample benefits election form and see what they sign up for.*

A favorite way for economists to gather honest feedback is to have people put their money where their mouth is — and actually pay for the options they want. Often they will give (or "pay") people money as part of the experiment, and see where they allocate it. Another approach is to restrict the number of "yeses" that people can give to a list of proposed and current benefits, so employees are faced with the need to *give up* existing benefits in order to get new ones.

Assess Behavioral Fit

Looking beyond whether your employees want a program, it's also important to assess whether they realistically would use it. Improving benefits usage is obviously a major focus of this entire book, but there are a few questions that can help you forecast usage *beforehand*:

- ❖ What do your employees do in their everyday lives that's relevant to the benefit or behavior?

- ❖ Are the behaviors you're proposing new and unusual?

For example, if a wellness program requires that employees wear an exercise tracker, are employees familiar with pedometers? Or have they not worn anything on their wrist since they were in high school sporting a Casio? If a new feature for the retirement package offers active accounts where employees can frequently reallocate and trade existing balances — do they do already trade their IRAs or other investments? Unlike asking people what benefits they *want* to have, you can safely ask them what they already *do* — since there is little incentive to misrepresent or be optimistic, a simple survey suffices.

Nothing appeals to everyone

For each behavior, think about the major groups of employees you have. Which groups of employees are likely to want to take the action or use the benefit, and which are likely to disregard it? Few programs can help everyone, so the question becomes: Does this program target the employees you really want to work with? For example, young, physically fit employees are going to respond differently to an appeal to walk 10,000 steps a day than employees who are clinically obese and have real difficultly moving around.

A Quick Recap

Next up, we will cover the crucial step of finding the right benefits intervention — a new program or change in an existing one — that meets company and employee needs. First, however, let's review what we've done so far.

1. **Define the outcome.** Make sure it's observable. Avoid states of mind like "knowing how to eat healthy" that fall short of the outcome you really care about. E.g., weight loss. Make sure to identify the target employees. Which subset of employees does the company particularly want or need to engage?

2. **Define potential actions.** What concrete actions might employees take that drives their outcomes?

3. **Know your employees.** Gather the information you already know about your employees, to see who is likely to want to use the program or take the particular action. Do some small tests with employees in which you see how they act in response to the benefit (instead of asking them how they *might* act).

5
CRAFTING THE INTERVENTION

You've listened to your employees and discovered what they want, and balanced their needs against the needs of the company. You've identified the concrete goals of the company — whether it be increased employee engagement, decreased cost, or lower levels of obesity.

Now it's time to examine concrete changes the HR team might make to their benefits offerings. Naturally, this is something that HR teams already do, often as part of an annual cycle. Here, we will review the particular behavioral implications for each option available to the HR team, and, add a few more options that aren't traditionally considered.

A *benefits intervention* is any change in the status quo that the HR team makes, in order to drive better benefits outcomes. It may turn out that the best way to achieve a particular outcome is to roll out a new program. It may mean tweaking an existing program. It may require a simple email highlighting an existing, but underutilized program, or an event to build a community of people around a program (like an exercise program). Each of these is a possible benefits intervention.

Changes made to benefit programs are often segmented into three very different areas: selecting the programs themselves, fine-tuning the design parameters, and implementing the programs effectively with employees. Here, we'll intentionally examine the challenge holistically, drawing upon both plan design and benefits implementation. We're looking for whatever tool can ensure employer and employee needs are met, as cost-effectively as possible.

In the previous chapter, we identified actions that employees might take that support their own, and the company's, goals. (For example, to support the goals of increased employee health and decreased employer cost, employees might invest in HSAs, exercise more, or smoke less.) What can employers actually do to accomplish these goals? There are six strategic types of benefits interventions companies can make to the design and workings of their programs:

1. Defaulting & Automation

2. Financial Incentives

3. Channel Factors

4. Promotion Campaigns

5. Education Campaigns

6. Changing the Benefits Lineup

Some, but not all, of these interventions are already familiar to HR practitioners. Changing the lineup, the financial incentives, and the promotion campaign are standard tools in the HR toolkit, to which behavior research can add a few insights. Defaulting and automation have been employed in limited circumstances, such as 401(k) auto-enrollment, but have many more unexplored possibilities. Channel factors are rarely discussed in the HR literature, but as we'll see, can be tremendously powerful.

The Six Types of Interventions

Defaulting and Automation

What it is: The most common example of defaulting and automation in the benefits arena is 401(k) auto-enrollment. With auto-enrollment, employers default employees into their retirement plan, and then automatically deduct income from their paycheck to go towards the plan. Employees are able to opt-out of the program if they want to or can change the details of their participation.

In fact, auto-enrollment is one of the greatest success stories of behavioral economics. It was studied and promoted by researchers as a means to increase the retirement savings of employees, most of whom were (and still are) woefully undersaving for their retirement. In numerous studies, auto-enrollment has been shown to increase retirement plan participation rates to 90% or more of a population, overnight.

Where it's important: Beyond 401(k) auto-enrollment, defaulting and automation are ideal in situations where the employer or vendor can actually perform the work that's required on behalf of the employee. We see this most often with financial programs, even beyond retirement: For example, employers could default employees into an emergency savings plan or into making HSA contributions.

It's harder to envision defaulting with wellness programs — employers can't exercise for you. However, that doesn't mean it isn't possible. Employers can default employees into using smaller plates at the company cafeteria (placing the larger plates further behind the small ones). Employers can, and do, default employees into a health plan that fits the needs of most workers.

When can it be implemented: In most companies, changes to the default *enrollment* of employees and instituting automation (like employee contributions) can only occur once a year — at the start of a new plan year. However, smaller changes — like the default placement of plates in the cafeteria — could occur at any time.

Benefits and downsides: Defaulting and automation have a clear upside for benefits usage: They require very little, if any, positive action by employees. But, that is also their greatest weakness.

Because they lack positive action by employees, programs with defaults and automation often suffer from low employee buy-in. At HelloWallet, we frequently encounter stories of employees who were defaulted into a retirement plan, unbeknownst to them, who are asked what they want to do with the funds when they leave the company. Since these employees never committed to the program in the first place, they simple cash out their "retirement funds," paying a significant penalty along the way; the purpose of the program to encourage long-term retirement savings is defeated *because* of defaulting.

Defaulting and automation also shift the burden of work, and responsibility, to the employer. Employees are expected *not* to take action, baring exceptional circumstances. That makes the precise choice of the default selected by employers paramount — for example, most employees stay with the default contribution rate they are opted into.[58]

If the employer really knows what health plan is best for most workers, or what level of life insurance is appropriate for them, that isn't necessarily a problem. If not, the employer risks being blamed for placing workers in a benefit program that is inappropriate for them.

Financial Incentives

What is it: Financial incentives are the strict dollars and cents of a program. You can think about them in terms of two subtypes: structural incentives and conditional ones.

---

[58] Madrian and Shea (2001). The default selected by the employer also serves as a cue to employees as what is the *correct* contribution. I.e., it is implicit advice, in addition to benefiting from employee inertia.

❖ **Structural incentives** are ones that everyone faces because they are built into the program itself — like the cost of a health insurance plan.

❖ **Conditional incentives** depend on employee behavior — like the potential to receive a 401(k) match, or *decreased* health insurance costs for employees who enroll in a wellness program.

For an HSA program, for example, structural benefits include the hard-nosed dollar figures of tax benefits, and employees may conditionally receive a matching contribution. Structural costs of the program include fees paid by the employee to the asset manager of investment-oriented HSAs or conditional costs include tax penalties for inappropriate use or early distribution.

HR practitioners often have a great deal of control over financial incentives. In many benefits arenas — such as medical, dental, and retirement programs — determining the specific fee structure and employer contribution for the policy is a big part of the HR practitioner's job.

The most extreme financial incentive is an employer mandate: Employees will be fired or risk problems on the job if they don't comply.

Where it's important: When automation isn't possible, structural incentives set the stage for the employee's choice to use a program or not. The financial costs and benefits of a program are essential for making the honest case to employees that participation is in their interest; it's hard to sell a program that costs employees more than they receive!

When can it be implemented: Most companies would only change structural incentives at the start of a new plan year. Changes in conditional incentives can theoretically be made at any time — especially if the incentive is small (e.g., an iPad) and doesn't require separate budget approval.

Benefits and downsides: Where automation isn't used, structural incentives are simply a necessity; employers must make choices there. The benefits are clear: All else being equal, the less something costs (or the more that people are paid to participate), the more likely it is that employees will do it. At the extreme end, there is a well-studied phenomenon that once something valuable becomes free,[59] people jump to try it out.[60] The bump in participation that happens when the price goes from $100 to FREE is generally much larger than the bump in participation caused by the price going from $200 to $100. In reverse, the more an employee has to pay for a benefit, the less likely it is that they will sign up for it, all else being equal.

Conditional incentives also have a clear upside — they work; if you pay someone enough to do something they will generally do it. In a review of 44 experimental studies that tested the impact of conditional financial incentives on preventative health behaviors, 73% of them did change individual behavior.[61] They were particularly effective for clear, short-run goals; less so for diffuse general goals.

The downsides are threefold. For *conditional usage incentives*, incentivizing employee participation isn't necessarily cost effective to the employer. When both decreasing employee cost (health insurance subsidies for anti-smoking programs) and increasing financial rewards to employees (HSA match contributions), the employer usually pays the difference. If the goal is to narrowly encourage usage among those who need the benefit, there are often free or less-costly ways to accomplish the same goal — in fact, all of the other techniques discussed here are examples.[62]

---

[59] This only works if the person still believes the thing is valuable after it becomes free. The price of an activity also serves as a signal for quality — so, without other information about value, free can simply tell people that the activity is worthless. So, the ideal situation is one in which the program is free to the employee, but costs non-employees a lot of money.

[60] See *Predictably Irrational* by Dan Ariely (2008)

[61] See Kane et al. (2004).

[62] There are also creative ways to structure the financial incentive that make it possible to decrease the cost to the company. Lotteries, in which employees have a chance to win a significant prize, are one route. They have been used in weight loss (Volpp et al. 2008) and savings (Tufano 2008)

Often, we don't have such narrow goals, however, especially with *structural incentives*. Instead, benefits are part of the total rewards packages available to employees; they attract and retain talent, and compensate employees for their hard work. Lowering the cost of a health insurance premium for everyone may not be a cost-effective way to increase health insurance *usage,* but it is an excellent way to reward employees. It's effectively a financial transfer between the company and employees, and should be evaluated separately from usage or behavioral goals.

The second downside with financial incentives is that they tend to "crowd out" other employee motivations. In short, the general rule is that when you pay someone to do something, they become less likely to do it on their own. I.e., when you provide an incentive to do a wellness survey, then take later remove it, expect participation to drop precipitously. In *Predictably Irrational,* Dan Ariely describes how individuals keep track of a financial and a non-financial "economy"; once you start talking about payment for action, any social bonds and relationships are thrown out the window.

Finally, the third downside to financial incentives is that they are relatively narrow tools. When you pay someone to do something, like taking a wellness survey, don't expect them to spontaneously start exercising more or *acting* on the results of that survey. I've seen so many retirement and wellness programs, in particular, kick off an education program with an incentive to participate in Week 1, then falter when the incentive doesn't apply to activities in Weeks 2, 3, or 4.

Given these downsides, are financial incentives a bad idea in the benefits context? No, absolutely not. Later in this chapter, we'll outline cases in which they are exactly the right tool to use. The take-away should be different: Financial incentives are only one tool in the HR practitioner's toolbox; and a truly effective benefits leader is skilled in using all the tools at his or her disposal.

---

contexts, for example. Many thanks to Charles DeSantis for referring me to the weight-loss work.

Channel Factors

What is it: Behavioral economics exists because narrow financial incentives aren't enough to explain why people act the way they do. One of the most startling findings from behavioral research is that "channel factors," or seemingly inconsequential characteristics of the environment in which one makes a decision, can have enormous impacts on behavior.[63]

Which small details of a benefit program shape whether employees use them? Based on our experimental research at HelloWallet, they are many: Everything from the sender of a message announcing the benefit, to the color of the button people click to set up their retirement contributions.

Small details aren't small in their effects — we've regularly seen 50% to 100% swings in participant behavior when changing minor details of a benefits communication.

While a wide diversity of details matter, two lessons researchers have drawn are about the importance of friction and anchors:

❖ Anything that annoys, delays, or makes employees do unnecessary work while signing up for or using a benefit, *could* be an important channel factor.[64] For example, online marketers have shown how each additional click required for someone to make a purchase usually decreases the likelihood that they will actually do so. By extension, with

---

[63] See for example Mullainathan and Shafir (2009) on minor changes affecting savings decisions.

[64] It's not a hard and fast rule. In fact, there are clearly the cases where the opposite is at work. Losing the most weight in a Biggest Loser Competition isn't easy — it's full of difficulty and frictions all the way along; however, it's the challenge itself that drives some employees to participate.

each additional screen or page in an open enrollment process, expect less employee attention and energy.[65]

❖ In many numerical decisions, people are unduly affected by the first value they see.[66] They take that initial value as a reference point or *anchor*, and then select their answer by adjusting relative to that anchor. The problem is that value of the anchor affects where the person ends up. For example, if you ask employees how much they would like to contribute, and provide an anchor like "for example, 3%", they will contribute much less than if you'd said "for example, 8%". Your example may have nothing to do with their retirement needs, but it will still affect what they contribute (so, choose your anchors carefully).

Where it's important: Channel factors are particularly relevant to the plan design and delivery process after core design choices have been made. I.e., after the team has decided whether individuals will be defaulted in, and decided the financial costs and benefits of the program to employees. They affect the moment of interaction, when employees decide about and use the benefit (or not):

1) The design and wording of communications to employee about the benefit.

2) The information architecture of the benefits portal (how information is structured across the site and how employees navigate it) or benefits pamphlet.

3) The detailed design of the page or paper on which people sign up for the benefit.

---

[65] I have yet to see a rigorous study of the per-click impact of additional screens in an open enrollment website, unfortunately. However, anecdotal evidence abounds.

[66] In fact, the "first value they see" could be completely unrelated to the task at hand, and still influence the person's choice. Famous results include a random number affecting subsequent judgments about the number of African countries in the UN (Tversky and Kahneman 1974) and how much people are willing to pay for goods, affected by awareness of their social security number (Ariely et al. 2003).

4) The detailed process by which employees reengage with the benefit — how they submit their FSA reimbursement requests, rebalance their retirement accounts, or attend the wellness program's exercise classes.

When can it be implemented: In most cases, companies can adjust the channel factors leading up to a benefit at any time — assuming their IT team and/or vendors can make the change.

Benefits and downsides: Behavioral economics shows us that the small details matter — immensely. In fact, fixing channel factors that block employees from using their benefits can be the most cost-effective way to improve the impact of a benefit program. By changing such small details as the day of week when messages are sent about a benefit, employers can have just as much impact on uptake as increasing the match rate for a retirement plan.[67]

Unfortunately, behavioral economics doesn't really provide a clear guide as to *which* details matter, and how much. There are countless small details, and they can be overwhelming to the uninitiated. While there are some tips (remove frictions to action), more is needed. One approach to take is to look for the specific obstacles that a set of employees faces in using its benefits and addressing them with as small of a change as possible.

In fact, the next chapter demonstrates how specific small changes gleaned from the research literature can improve usage. It provides a guide so that the myriad of potentially important details don't become overwhelming. First however, let's address the other big approaches that employers can use to drive benefits usage.

Promotion Campaigns

What is it: When the benefits offering is ready to go, employers need to inform employees about it. That marketing effort may be a simple email, posters in the break room, a social media campaign, or a formal launch event with all staff in attendance.

---

[67] Based on experiments conducted at HelloWallet.

Where it's important: From a behavioral perspective, the promotion of a benefit has two distinct impacts: It gets people's attention, and it offers employees with one way to *think* about the benefit. As mentioned in Chapter 2, we need to be *cued* to think about taking action. We have too many other things to do in our lives to spontaneously start thinking about a new benefit program. Once that cue occurs, a slew of cognitive processes are triggered — an intuitive reaction, an analysis of costs and benefits, an assessment of urgency, etc. The promotion effort shapes that reaction, and makes employees aware of the relevant costs and benefits.

Employers have tremendous opportunity (and responsibility) to drive usage through good promotion. For example, with an HSA program, employers could highlight:

❖ The tax-benefits of HSA contributions

❖ The risk of not having enough money for medical expenses or retirement

❖ The piece of mind of having a cushion of medical savings

❖ The removal of temptation to spend their medical savings on other things that an HSA's legal restrictions provide.

When can it be implemented: Any time! That is one of the best features of promotion campaigns.

Benefits and downsides: Thankfully, the impact that benefits promotion has on employee usage is not directly tied to the *cost* of that effort. A simple set of emails can be just as effective as a massive awareness raising campaign for telling people about a new program — depending on how each of them is executed in practice.

Promotional efforts are subject to many of the channel factors discussed previously — very small details matter immensely. As mentioned before, that is both a boon and a bane for employers.

Education Campaigns

One area where further attention generally *isn't* needed is employee education. Not because employees already know all of the relevant details about their benefits, or, at the other extreme, employees aren't listening, so education efforts are wasted. Rather, from a *behavioral* perspective, there's considerable evidence that educating people about a decision has surprisingly little impact on what they actually do.

A prime example in the benefits arena comes from financial literacy education programs. Financial literacy programs, such as education seminars about the importance of retirement savings or how compound interest functions over time, were long promoted as an important way to improve the financial habits of Americans. However, when they were tested with more rigorous methods, the results were disappointing — little to no impact on behavior.[68]

Here's why. When it comes to education efforts, the people that voluntarily attend are often those who are most interested. As a retirement professional put it: "At a baseball game, you expect to find baseball fans, right?" — and so you shouldn't be surprised that when you invite people to a finance topic, the ones who come are the ones who are already interested and thus the *least* likely to change their behavior because of it.

Second, most employees, at a basic level, already understand what their benefit programs do. They may not know the ins and outs of the programs — the health care fee structures, the optimal scenarios for each plan — but they already know enough to judge whether it's right for them. Further information may strengthen that view, but by and large it isn't going to fundamentally change their *behavior*. Often, something else blocks them from taking action — and that something else may be a lack of time, resources, or confidence. Education per se isn't the problem.

---

[68] See Mandell and Klein (2009) for example on the (null) effect of financial literacy education in high schools on subsequent behavior.

Where it's important: Education efforts are most important when the benefit is truly new — like nothing the employee has seen before. In other words, for fresh-out-of-school employees and for completely new programs like health exchanges. And, even then, the basics that most employees will use to actually determine their behavior can nicely fit on a flyer.

When can it be implemented: Any time.

Changing the Benefits Lineup

What is it: This intervention is the most straightforward of them all — it entails adding or removing programs from the suite of benefits offered to employees, or changing which employees are eligible for a benefit.[69]

Where it's important: Companies may have many reasons for changing their basic lineup, but from a behavioral perspective this is most important when there is a fundamental mismatch between company goals or employee needs identified in the last chapter, and the current lineup. In other words:

1. **Adding a benefit:** When none of the existing benefits can cost effectively meet a need. I.e., when employees simply do not have access to something they desire and that benefits the company.

2. **Removing a benefit:** When there is no longer an employee need or a company goal that is met by the program.

3. **Changing the provider of a benefit:** When a more cost-effective option is found, or employees simply don't have access to a key feature of the new benefit program. For example, the current dental plan does not cover the employee's preferred dentists.

---

[69] Since, from the perspective of the individual employee, changing whether something is offered to the company as a whole, or offered to them or not, is effectively the same thing.

When can it be implemented: Realistically, companies usually change the benefits lineup at the start of a new plan year (or the start of a new calendar year, if different).

Benefits and downsides: Changing the lineup has the obvious benefit of aligning the current offerings to company goals. If a program is no longer needed (and used), there are clear cost savings. If a program is common among competing companies, and prospective employees like it, then it has clear benefits for attracting and retaining talent. And so forth — there aren't any unique insights inspired by the behavioral research about which programs a company should or should not have.

In terms of usage, however, changing providers or adding a new complementary program is the *last* option that companies should consider if employees are not using a desirable benefit. That is because changing providers has significant costs that can be avoided by cheaper methods. Defaulting, incentives, channel factors, promotion campaigns, and to a much lesser extent, education campaigns can all increase usage of the benefit without incurring the administrative costs of searching for new providers, vetting them, and paying for set-up and implementation.

Tips on Where to Start

While there are no hard and fast rules, here are scenarios in which certain behavioral approaches are known to be very effective. In this section, let's draw out each of these "special scenarios" that was mentioned above. When designing a new benefits package, or updating the design of an existing one, check if any of these scenarios apply:

First, there are the two questions of basic access.

1. Is there no way that the company can meet an identified need with the current lineup? Then add a program or change providers for existing programs.

2. Is a program underutilized, and the company does not have a compelling reason to encourage usage? Drop it.

If a program is *available* to employees, but underutilized, then:

1. Is automation possible and employee engagement not required? Use defaulting and automation to boost usage and impact.

2. Is the program something employees would normally buy, but it's possible to make the program free to the employee? If so, do it. Getting something (you really want) for free motivates people like nothing else.

3. Is there a clear moment of friction that interferes with employees signing up for, or using the benefit? If so, try to remove that channel factor.

4. Does the employee only need to do the action once? If so, conditional incentives (paying people to do it!) can be quite cost effective.

5. Is the benefit program against the financial interest of employees? That is, does the company health plan cost more than they would get in ACA health exchanges, or is a voluntary benefit offered to employees, like pet insurance, really not a good deal relative to the open market? If so, fix the financial incentives — subsidize the cost, increase the benefits (e.g., match), or drop the benefit.

If you've responded "no" to all of the above, then sorry, there aren't any simple solutions. Instead, a detailed review of the particular behavioral obstacles, and how financial incentives, channel factors, and promotion campaigns can be used to overcome them, is required. We'll explore that in Chapter 8.

Selecting the Right Intervention

We now have a sense of what interventions are possible, and the scenarios in which they are particularly effective. Let's return to the problem of finding the right intervention for a particular set of employee and employer goals.

In the last chapter, we:

1. **Defined the outcome** that the company seeks — a more engaged workforce, decreased cost, increased health, etc.

2. **Define potential actions,** that employees *might* take to drive those outcomes — such as signing up for an HSA, exercising more, or smoking less.

3. **Gathered knowledge about the employees,** to see which actions employees *want* to take, such as exercising more.

With that list of potential actions, excluding those that employees are unlikely to agree to, what does the employer actually do to support action? Is a new benefit program needed, a change in the incentives of an existing one, or are simple improvements to the frictions and promotion of the program needed? For that, we should brainstorm options for benefits interventions.

Brainstorming Options

List out possible benefits interventions that the team can make. Some interventions are obvious — for employee wellness, for example, there are already a range of vendor programs. Put them down on the list. But, we're also looking for non-obvious interventions. In particular,

❖ *What is the simplest, most straightforward action your team could take?* Send an email about an existing wellness program on the books? Tell them about the gym down the street, even if it isn't company sponsored?

❖ *What changes can you make to an existing program that might accomplish the outcome?* For wellness, is it a change in the reimbursement rate for preventive care services?

❖ *How can you increase engagement with an existing program without changing it?* Perhaps you can organize a speaker series at your company, in which people who've already used and benefited from the program can share their stories and ask others to commit to join as well?

❖ *What new programs are available that might get the job done?* Is there a fancy new exercise program with a Bluetooth-enabled tracker and mobile app? Or a simple workplace wellness program with an in-person coach?

As before, we're building a list — we're not critiquing it yet. Some of these interventions will be cost-prohibitive; some will be ineffective. We'll separate the wheat from the chaff shortly. We're trying to open up the process enough so that we can *jump benefits silos.*

Jumping Silos

For senior HR managers, thinking about target outcomes and a range of possible employee behaviors opens up an opportunity: to holistically analyze benefits challenges and identify the right intervention to solve it, even if that means jumping benefits silos. There are two ways to do this:

1. **A different type of benefit program may solve the problem more effectively.** In the example above, I mentioned a company that is losing prospective employees because they see the retirement benefits as stingy.

   If what the company really cares about is attracting high quality workers, then it isn't (necessarily) a retirement benefits problem at all. An increase in salary, or other perks, could more than offset any negative perception of the retirement benefits, for a net gain to both the company and the new hires. I.e., you can meet the needs of employees and attract, retain, and motivate more effective if you are thinking about *outcomes* first, and *benefits* silos second.

2. **A new program, or even a change to the design of an existing one, may not be needed at all.** Imagine a retirement program with a low participation rate. Instead of launching a new financial literacy campaign or changing the match rates and eligibility criteria, there are other options that can be more cost-effective. Many HR leaders already

know about the power of auto-enrollment to boost participation. In addition, large impacts can be found by simply requiring that employees state whether or not they will enroll in the plan, or by leveraging "loss aversion", by highlighting the loss of unused match dollars in internal communications.

In both cases, look broadly for benefits interventions — any change in the suite of benefits and communications that might work. Next up, let's what we know about the employee base, so we can better match company and employee needs with these benefits interventions.

Making the Call

By this point, you should have a list of potential benefits interventions (e.g., free exercise classes, BMI incentives, or success stories from dieters), based on the particular outcome your company seeks to reach (e.g., healthier employees) and the employees' behaviors that drive that outcome (e.g., exercising more or dieting). You should also have information about your employees — whether they are generally interested in the intervention, how *normal* the behavior is for them already, and which major groups of employees might benefit the most (and least) from the program. Now it's time to winnow down the list and find one or more interventions that seem the most promising.

You can evaluate potential benefits intervention according to timing criteria:

1. **Impact**: How well will the intervention actually achieve the target outcome?

2. **Ease**: How difficult is it for employees to take action?

3. **Cost**: How costly will it be for the company to deploy that intervention?

4. **Fit**: Does the intervention make sense for the company's larger goals and culture?

5. **Timing:** When does an intervention need to occur, and is it feasible given the type of intervention and time of year?

Let's use an employee weight-loss example:

❖ Buying a "magic" diet pill for all employees may be very impactful, and easy for people to take, but tremendously costly for the company.

❖ Changing the cafeteria around to make healthier options more prominent may be impactful and not very costly for the company, but it doesn't fit the company's larger goals of making a big statement about health and showing employees that the company cares.

There's no hard and fast rule on how to weigh each of these five criteria; it depends on the needs of the company and the resources available.

Remember, Define Success and Failure Upfront

After you've selected the intervention you'd like to use, it's useful to look again at the outcome, and make sure you have clarity around what success and failure mean, given the benefits intervention. This is especially true if the intervention is a vendor program; before engaging in a vendor discussion about a program, first ask: What is it that *you* want from a program? What's the gap your team or other employees identified in the current benefits offering? What is the cost or standardization goal you have in mind for your next benefits move?

One way of clarifying this is to answer three simple questions:

1. What outcome do I want to accomplish?

2. How will I determine success?

3. How will I determine failure?

For example, let's say you have a target of increasing the HSA enrollment among those who are eligible, in-between open enrollment periods:

1. **Outcome**: Increase HSA enrollment among eligibles.

2. **Success**: Move from current 15% level to 50% of employees.

3. **Failure**: Anything less than 25% of employees enrolled.

Here's another very different example. Let's say you have a target of standardizing insurance offerings. In the past, you've had 30 different plans, offered in some regions and not others, with significant overlap in certain regions.

1. **Outcome**: Standardize plan offerings to decrease administrative costs.

2. **Success**: Two to four offerings per region.

3. **Failure**: This is a bit more complex. Clearly, you can fail to decrease the number of programs. But there are other possible downsides to consider. For example, employee complaints go up, or consolidated plan costs increase to the employer and/or employee.

Jump Ahead

If you've decided that what you really need is to promote or educate around an existing benefits offering, without major changes to how the program works, then you can jump ahead to the "Implementation" phase of the process. That starts in Chapter 8. Chapters 6 and 7 cover additional issues when Crafting the core design of the benefits package, and Testing assumptions about how the program will run.

A Quick Recap

❖ **There are six types of interventions** that employers can make on their benefits, to drive beneficial outcomes for the employer and employee. Obviously, employers can change the lineup or change the financial incentives for existing programs. Less obviously, employers can cleverly use defaulting and automation, address frictions or other "channel factors" that impede employees, or use behavioral techniques to invigorate the promotion of the benefit.

❖ **Defaulting and automation,** such as 401(k) auto-enrollment are incredibly powerful where employee buy-in is not required.

❖ **Channel factors** are seemingly inconsequential aspects of the environment in which employees decide about their benefits that greatly shape those choices. For example: The number of clicks employees are required to make or the positioning of text and buttons on the screen. The details matter — the problem is that it's not always clear *which* details. Chapters 8-10 address that.

❖ **Brainstorm multiple possible interventions,** intentionally looking for non-obvious and minimally invasive and costly routes to achieve the same usage and impact goals.

❖ **Evaluate the possible options** based on their impact for the company and employee, likelihood that employees will actually use them, cost to the company, and fit with the company culture.

❖ **Define success and failure before implementing anything** — to save the team disagreements, and wasted effort later on.

6

SPECIAL FOCUS: EVALUATING VENDOR PROGRAMS

"A long-running and well-respected workplace wellness program at PepsiCo that encourages employees to adopt healthier habits has not reduced healthcare costs, according to the most comprehensive evaluation of such a program ever published."[70]

No company wants a headline like that one, which ran in Reuters recently and covered a seven-year, rigorous scientific study of PepsiCo's wellness program. This chapter is about how ensure the programs that your company spends good money on actually work as advertised.

---

[70] Begley (2014). PepsiCo had the courage to test its program — something we'll talk about in this chapter and later on. Unfortunately, many companies simply take it on faith that their programs work, and end up throwing away benefits funds without ever knowing it and correcting course.

In Chapters 4 and 5, we looked at how to analyze the particular needs of employees and match them to potential *benefits interventions* — i.e., anything from a new benefit program to a new communications program around an existing benefit program. When the intervention entails rolling out a new program — whether it be an in-house program or a vendor-supplied one, then HR teams have the opportunity and duty to dig into the available data and evaluate what they really mean.

Is the Evidence Solid?

Imagine Company X, which recently started offering a high-deductible health care plan, and is evaluating potential HSA administrators. The company is concerned about how poorly prepared its employees seem to be for medical expenses, and how little engagement they have with their healthcare over all. HSAs are a promising a route to improve healthcare engagement and financial preparation at the same time.

As the company evaluates HSA administrators, the vendors offer enticing information about their programs. Many combine the simple administration of funds with an online platform for employee engagement and expense planning, educational material for employees, and guidance on how to design employer contributions and match formulas.

A survey run by one of the HSA administrators, Xerox's BenefitWallet, shows that a whopping 81% of respondents "strongly agree/agree having an HSA is valuable to them," and similar numbers of respondents see the tax advantages as "extremely" or "very" important.[71] More than one-half said they are putting aside *more money than before* the HSA for their healthcare costs, 29% said that they are talking with their doctors about the real cost of care, and a vital 13% are more actively managing their chronic diseases.[72]

---

[71] See Xerox HR Solutions (2013)

[72] BenefitWallet 2013 Member Survey. Stonehouse (2013). For original study, see Xerox HR Solutions (2013)

Another HSA administrator, HSA Bank, offers evidence about how employees enrolled in HSAs are more active healthcare consumers: They are more likely to know the costs of care, select lower-cost treatment options, and request lower-cost generic drugs when available. The administrator provides easy online tools for employees, shows how much employees (and employers) can save on medical expenses, and helps employers with program design and employee education. [73]

Across the range of potential vendors, Company X encounters information about direct tax savings, indirect medical insurance savings, improved employee engagement, and improved employee health. They also see that vendors can provide significant support for the design and implementation of the programs, working with the HR team and directly with employees through trainings and their online platforms.

How can Company X actually choose whether to offer an HSA at all, and which vendor to go with? And, more broadly, how can an HR team sift through the competing promises and data about different programs to decide which ones are effective, and which ones are best suited for their employees?

Vendor selection is clearly a multifaceted and complex process, and there are numerous issues to consider — ranging from financial (employer cost and benefit), to organizational (employee engagement and wellness), to legal (compliance requirements and new regulations) to logistical (complexity of implementation, support from experts).

Books such as the *WorldAtWork Total Rewards Manual* cover many of the design and legal issues involved in vendor selection and plan design; those broader issues are beyond the scope of this book. Instead, our goal here is to focus in on particular lessons and techniques from the behavioral sciences that can help this process — complementing your HR team's existing expertise and empowering its members with new tools to select vendors effectively.

---

[73] See http://www.hsabank.com/~/media/files/employer_manual and http://www.hsabank.com/hsabank/employers/the-hsa-bank-advantage

What are we looking for?

From a behavioral perspective, there's one overriding question that benefits providers should answer about their programs:

Causal Impact: What is the *final outcome*, driven by observable changes in *employee behavior*, which was *caused by* the program?

Let's pick about the three core elements of this causal impact:

- ❖ **Final Outcome.** What does the program do that employers actually care about? If the employer cares about healthcare costs, what is the change in healthcare costs that the program provides?[74] Anything *else*, like surveys that say how much employees like the program, is useful if the goal is employee satisfaction, but irrelevant on the particular issue of healthcare costs.

- ❖ **Caused By.** Did the program cause the outcome, or is it something that would have happened on its own? In particular, did the program simply select people who were naturally engaged, healthy, etc., or did it help people become more engaged or healthy than they otherwise would have been?

- ❖ **Employee Behavior.** Since effective benefits mean behavior change, what do employees actually do differently? This is a useful way to double-check that the impact a program says it has it real — if it doesn't show up in changes in employee behavior, it usually can't affect real-world outcomes. Also, it's an opportunity to ask about the *means* of achieving that end: was the change in employee behavior voluntary and welcomed?

Naturally, vendors also should say how much the program costs, how long it will take to implement, what staffing resources are required within the company etc. — they are often much better at

---

[74] Usually, it won't be a simple dollar figure, but rather a formula or statistical model with probabilities of various outcomes — but the core idea is the same.

answering those questions than questions about causal impact. With knowledge about the causal impact in hand (and costs, timing, etc.) for each potential vendor, HR teams then select the program that best fits their own desired outcomes, as documented in the last chapter.

Why is causal impact so difficult to glean? Problems arise at two levels — methodology and incentives. Methodologically, it takes planning and thoughtful execution to measure how people behave *differently than they would have without the program*. It's not rocket science, but it takes a bit more work. In terms of incentives, vendors, and brokers/consultants don't necessarily have the incentive to put in that extra time and work — something that HR professionals have the power to change.

To better understand these challenges, let's take a deeper look at how programs are often pitched to prospective HR buyers.

Don't Believe (Most of) the Numbers

Simply put, most of the data that vendors and brokers/consultants provide about their programs aren't helpful in evaluating their impact. It's not that the vendors, brokers, and consultants are trying to hide something; the techniques used to show the effectiveness of most programs are flawed. As Al Lewis states, rather bluntly:

> *"Vendors routinely show you outcomes reports for your Population Health Improvement programs whose savings claims are much closer to fact than fiction." – Lewis (2012), pg. xiv*

In his book, *Why Nobody Believes the Numbers*, Lewis provides a humorous and often scathing look at how bad methodology leads to completely nonsensical impact numbers in the population health management field. If you're ever evaluating a population-based wellness program, it's an eye-opening read. While I unfortunately do not have his sense of humor, let's take a similar look at techniques used in the broader benefits arena.

Measuring It Incorrectly: Asking Employees about Impact

The simplest way to measure the impact of a program is to ask the participants. Unfortunately, the results are often completely misleading. Surveys, and similar approaches to directly asking participants what they think about a program like interviews and assessing company chatter, are flawed because of how they gather information. To make things concrete, let's continue the HSA example above, and assume a vendor runs a survey asking HSA participants about its program.

Problem: People who answer the question are different from those who don't

In most surveys, substantially less than 100% of the people you ask to complete the survey (or interview, or focus group, etc.) actually do so. The people who choose to answer are *different* than those who don't. For example, people who are likely to answer a survey about their HSA are more likely to know about their HSA and use it than those who don't answer the survey. So, if you see a survey that shows that people are really engaged with their HSA, or with any benefit program, it shouldn't be surprising — because you're simply not hearing from the people who *aren't* engaged.

Technical Name: Non-response bias

How serious can it be: Widely misleading. Example: you ask employees about their interest in a program. The 10 employees who are interested respond, and say yes. The other 90 don't respond. Instead of the real 10% level of interest, you'd see a 100% interest level with that survey.

What to look for: Any time there is an optional request for personal information and substantially less than 100% of people respond to the request. This is especially a problem when the survey is related to engagement, awareness, interest, or support for a program.

Can it be fixed: Yes, there are sophisticated methods to correct for non-response bias. But, I've rarely seen vendors use them. If you ask your vendor/broker how they correct for non-response bias, and they give you a blank stare, they didn't correct for it. In most cases, it's easier to look for a better source of data (like employee behavior) than it is to correct for non-response bias.

Problem: People stretch the truth

If you hold an educational workshop about HSAs, then ask participants if the information was useful for them, many of them (assuming they don't hate you), are going to say "yes". Even if the participants were actually asleep or couldn't understand the presentation. Why? Because that's the socially acceptable thing to say.

Similarly, there are numerous other biases in which people stretch the truth — when they say what they want to be true ("of course I'll go to the gym next year"), when they try to be consistent with previous statements ("sure, I *still* think HSAs are great"), or when they say yes just to be agreeable to get done with the survey.

Technical Name: Social Desirability Bias and others, including acquiescence bias and a consistency motif[75]

What to look for: When you can reasonably guess what people will say just by reading the question and not knowing them

Can it be fixed: Yes, but it's hard. Look for better data.

Problem: People don't know the answer

Beyond stretching the truth, often people simply don't know the answer to the question — but they'll answer anyway. With benefits surveys, this is especially true if you ask about changes in behavior and why people do it.

Much of our daily behavior is outside of conscious control. Almost 50% of our behavior is habitual,[76] and other behaviors, like scanning and discarding information about one's benefits, are also

---

[75] See Podsakoff et al. (2003)
[76] See Wood et al. (2002); Dean (2013)

"nonconscious": If we don't detect an immediately relevant cue for action or have a negative intuitive reaction, and the idea doesn't even bubble up to conscious awareness. Nevertheless, when our behavior is nonconscious, our conscious minds try to understand what we're doing — and so, it makes up stories. Those stories are convincing — to ourselves and others — but simply not true. So, asking someone why they are seeing the doctor more often may simply get you an answer that *sounds* good to their conscious mind, but has nothing to do with the real causes.

We're also not very good at *remembering* specifics about or frequencies of our own behavior, especially when it is occurs over a long period of time or changes slowly.[77] We remember novel, extreme, and recent events; things that are similar over time which we compress into "prototypical" memories. (Can you remember exactly how you made breakfast four years and 126 days ago?) So, questions that ask us the frequency of irregular events ("How often did you see the doctor in the last year?") or slow changes over time ("Are you going to the doctor more than we were before?") tax the limits of our memory. Our conscious minds will make up an answer, but who knows if it's right?[78]

Technical Names: Interpreter theory; Dual process theory; Autobiographical Memory[79]

What to look for: Any questions asking people to remember the frequency of events, or why they changed their behavior in the past.

Can it be fixed: Not really. This data can be gathered only through observation.

---

[77] E.g., Draaisma (2013)

[78] And, perhaps even more importantly — these made-up answers are easily biased by our environment. If we're answering a survey about HSAs, and we have no idea about how often we've been to the doctor, we'll use the fact that we're doing a survey as a *clue* that we went more (or less, depending on how you feel about HSAs).

[79] See Kahneman (2011), Draaisma (2013) for two of the many books on dual process theory and autobiographical memory, respectively.

Measuring It Incorrectly: Observing Impact

Instead of *asking* people what they think about a program, we can (and should) observe what they actually do. For example, instead of asking people how much they've walked every day, we can track it automatically with pedometers, used in wellness programs like Virgin Pulse, or with mobile-phone apps like Moves.

Ultimately, that is the type of data you want from your vendors — automatically tracked, unambiguous information about whether employees are succeeding or not with their program. But, there are pitfalls here, too.

Problem: Pre/Post Analyses Don't Look At Outside Influences

It seems quite natural to look at employee behavior before a program is rolled out, and after, and then compare the results. For example: to look at how much people are saving for medical expenses before the HSA was rolled out, and afterwards. However, a major challenge arises in figuring out whether the HSA caused any changes, or something else did.

Let's say you measured medical savings before the HSA program and six months after rollout, and found that people had $100 more in savings, on average. That's great, right? Maybe. Perhaps it's just the time of year — parents expecting babies during peak summer birth months[80] may be saving up money and others may be saving more because winter illnesses (flu, etc.) are over. Or, maybe it's because a completely different wellness program at the company was encouraging people to live healthier and so employees didn't *spend* as much as they'd thought for medical expenses.

Similar problems arise with other benefits. If you see 401(k) contributions increase after a new education program, is it because of the program — or because employees just got a bonus? If you see employee satisfaction increase over the last few months, is it because of a new workplace engagement program, or because it's sunnier

---

[80] http://www.livescience.com/32728-baby-month-is-almost-here-.html

outside?[81] Each individual example you can look into and potentially remove as an explanation; the challenge lies in discovering all of the *unknown*, hidden events that might have happened at the same time.

Technical Name: Extraneous factors (and numerous other names)

What to look for: The phrase "before and after" in any data analysis

Can it be fixed: Yes, with complex statistical models and detailed data about individuals and their environment. This approach doesn't appear to be used often, however, in most pre/post analyses by vendors.

Problem: Comparing Users of a Program versus Non-Users

Since pre/post analyses are often flawed, a natural response is to look at people at the same point in time — those who enrolled in a benefit program versus those who didn't. That's great, except that the two groups of people are probably very different from one another, and for reasons that have nothing to do with the program.

Using the HSA example, how would you expect people who have an HSA to be different than those who don't? Employees who took action and decided to sign up and contribute are probably more active and engaged generally than those who didn't take action. It's a very similar problem to the one we discussed above about non-response bias (employees who choose to answer your survey are different than those who don't).

In addition, enrollees and non-enrollees may be different for structural reasons. For example, maybe the company only switched non-union employees to a high-deductible, HSA-eligible plan while the union employees are under a different health care plan. If the union employees have different job titles and demographics than the non-union employees, any analysis that compared their healthcare usage (and assumed it was because of the HSA) would be flawed.

Technical Name: Selection Effects; "Population effects"

---

[81] Schwarz and Clore (1983)

What to look for: The magic phrase "we compared enrollees versus non-enrollees"

Can it be fixed: Yes, with careful statistical matching techniques and copious data about individuals. I'll discuss this approach in more detail below.

Problem: Sometimes it's intentional

Thus far, I've assumed the best about vendors, brokers, and benefits consultants. I've assumed that the problems are fundamentally ones of method, and not of malice. We know in our hearts that sometimes, something else is going on, and the vendor (and perhaps the broker) is cherry picking: selecting information that puts the program in a good light and discarding conflicting information, or simply making up numbers that sound good.

I won't try to estimate how often this occurs (see Lewis's *Why Nobody Believes the Numbers* for a cynical take). But, there are some good rules of thumb that can help you stay on solid ground, and avoid intentional and unintentional problems:

- ❖ The more complex the analysis, the more opportunity for confusion

- ❖ There must be a comparison group that is the same as the group that received the benefit program

- ❖ Watch out for vendors who aren't willing to share the data or underlying analysis

- ❖ It's easier to be fooled, intentionally or unintentionally, with analyses that only look at the benefits of a program, or the people who were *helped* by it

- ❖ It's harder to make errors in the analysis if there is an external, third-party review

- ❖ Watch out if the metrics used to show the benefit of the program keep switching over time.

I'm a stats guy, and I've seen lots of funny things over the years. It really doesn't matter whether the errors are intentional or unintentional — the real question is whether you can trust the results. You don't need to be an expert in statistics to do it. These rules of thumb, and the other tips in this chapter, are tools to help you ramp up your already well-exercised B.S. detector when it comes to benefits impact numbers. Next up, we'll look at another problem that should set off your alarm bells: exciting, but irrelevant, metrics.

Measuring the Wrong Thing

In the last section, we talked about what can go awry when the wrong methods are used.[82] But, an even more straightforward problem occurs when vendors simply measure the wrong thing — when they aren't actually measuring and telling you about the final outcome that you care about.

> *Employee participation and comparable offerings by other companies are almost always the wrong metrics to use.*

While HR teams are accustomed to looking at metrics such as employee participation, satisfaction, and benchmarks within an industry, usually they just aren't that important on their own. They are instead what vendors (by default) offer, and HR teams use them as a *proxy* for the value programs provide. Unfortunately, they can be very misleading — the fact that most large companies have some type of wellness program doesn't mean they actually work, and there's good evidence that many programs don't.[83] HR can, and should demand more — the real impact on employees.

Let's dig into some of these problems in greater detail.

Problem: Participation Metrics

In Chapter 3, we talked about the importance of identifying and documenting the outcomes that your company really cares about.

---

[82] We'll talk about better, more reliable methods, shortly.

[83] See Begley's (2014) high profile example of Pepsi's long-running program that didn't work as advertised. There's also evidence that financial literacy programs may not work as advertised (e.g., Mandell and Klein 2009) nor do many population health improving programs (Lewis 2012)

Your company may want to roll out an HSA to help your employees be financially prepared for medical emergencies; they may believe strongly in employee engagement with the healthcare system; or, they may roll it out to improve their own bottom line and save on FICA taxes. Yet, "participation" in a program is so often what we see touted about a program.

Whatever your company's goal is, it's probably not *mere participation*. If all your company is hoping for is for people to sign up for the program, that's OK. For everyone else, watch out — don't assume that participation is a good proxy for actual outcomes and changes in behavior. The main reason why participation numbers (alone) are suspect is simple: **Participation numbers are easy to fudge.**

The easiest way that vendors (and sometimes well-meaning companies) boost participation numbers is to offer an incentive: i.e., pay people to participate. If you pay someone enough money (or free stuff) to come to a wellness workshop, they will. Paying someone to attend an introductory event doesn't lead to long-term changes in behavior — in fact it can *decrease* long-term changes. We've talked more about the benefits and problems with incentives in Chapter 5.

Problem: Fuzzy Engagement Metrics

You'll often find vendors stating that their products encourage "employee engagement" — but what does that actually mean? Employee engagement is a tremendously fuzzy term, one that is thrown around for anything good and intangible about employee behavior — from greater productivity or creativity to loyalty to life satisfaction. In many cases, engagement just means participation in an event or opening/clicking on an email — and has the same problems listed above. We discussed engagement, what aspects are actually meaningful and useful for a company, and how (if at all) to improve it in Chapter 6.

In other cases, where engagement is something more meaningful than opening an email, one should still ask — is what this vendor means by "engagement" actually what the company cares about? Or is it a distraction?

Problem: Getting Distracted

Underneath participation and (many) engagement metrics are a more fundamental problem — distraction. Some vendors, faced with the complexities of measuring causal impact, highlight all of the "extras" that a program provides: Ready-made email templates, easy reporting, unified systems for administering multiple benefits at once, etc.[84] Or, they avoid discussion of real impact numbers and instead talk about how other companies are using it, adding similar benefits (and therefore so should you).[85] Proof that other companies have taken the leap and used a service is important, and shouldn't be dismissed. Similarly, easy program administration is great. But these are not substitutes for showing that the product actually works — that they cause changes in something that employees and the employer actually care about.

What Numbers Can You Trust?

With so many pitfalls facing you and your team in interpreting the promised impact of a benefit program, what can you really trust? There are in fact robust techniques that can assess the impact of a program. And while your team may not have the background to deploy them directly, your vendor should — especially since they are asking for your money!

There are three methods that are particularly powerful and relevant for assessing the value that a benefit program provides: experiments, statistical matching techniques, and measuring unique outcomes. In some cases, a vendor may already have this reliable, meaningful information about its program. If not though, that's not a death knell for the program — as long as they are willing to work with you to gather that data, and align their incentives accordingly. In this section, we'll review the three main (and reliable) sources of impact

---

[84] See, for example, Xerox's BenefitsWallet.

[85] See Metlife's Voluntary Benefits, for example https://www.metlife.com/business/benefit-products/voluntary-benefits/index.html

numbers, and how to work with vendors to get them if they don't already exist.

Experiments

Controlled, randomized experiments are used in everything from pharmaceutical trials to presidential political campaigns to determine what works and what doesn't.[86] When lives are on the line (real and political), experiments are what experts turn to. They are the gold standard to determine the causal impact of a program.

The idea behind experiments is simple: **Change something, measure something**. The key for experiments is that you change one and only one thing — the thing for which you want to understand impact. In the case of benefits, that means that the vendor needs to give the program to some people, and not to another set of people, who are otherwise identical, then measure the difference in outcomes between the two groups.

How can one be sure that people given the benefit program are the same as those who don't get the program? I.e., that the only thing that changes between the two groups is the program itself, and not something else about the people like their average age, income, etc.? You take a sufficiently large group of people, and then randomly assign them into the group that gets the program (the "treatment" group) or not (the "control" group). While each person is different, on average the two groups are exactly the same at the start of the program because of that random assignment process.

When the program is finished, then it's quite straightforward to measure the impact it has had:

Impact of Benefit program = Outcome for Group with Program - Outcome for Group with Without Program

That's it. You've probably noticed that I've been vague about exactly what "outcomes" and "programs" are being measured. That's because it actually doesn't matter. This approach works across wellness programs, retirement planning seminars, dental insurance,

---

[86] Issenberg (2010)

and pet care benefits. And, it works whether the company wants to measure employee health, retirement contributions or net cost to the company. Again, the technique is used in everything from evaluating surgical procedures to designing websites that sell shoes.[87]

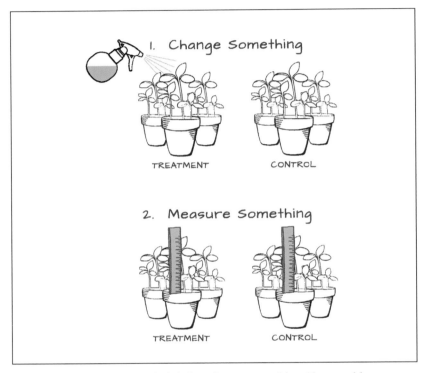

Figure 10: Experiments in brief — change something (the one thing you want to study) in one randomly selected group, and measure something (like employee outcomes) for both groups to compare them.

For the person designing the experiment (which should be the vendor or third-party researchers, and usually isn't someone on your HR team), there are some complexities to watch out for. First, the two groups need to be "large enough" for the experiment to give valid results; there are straightforward statistical tests that answer that question. Second, the selection between the two groups needs to

---

[87] See https://www.youtube.com/watch?v=FhHYHqJGrEA for a Zappos (shoes) example; see WhichTestWon.com for hundreds of other commercial examples.

be truly random — not just unknown. I.e., they need to figuratively flip a coin for each person and see which group they should be in.

From the perspective of an HR team, there are great benefits when vendors provide experimental data:

❖ **There's (usually) little interpretation involved; either the impact is there or it isn't.** As we discussed earlier, the more complex the analysis, the more likely it is that a vendor or broker will intentionally or unintentionally make a mistake or find a "good" data point that doesn't really fit the facts.

❖ **No need to rely on surveys or self-reported outcomes.** Measuring outcomes with experiments avoids the need to ask people what they *think* about a program, and avoids the opportunity for them to stretch the truth.

❖ **The people are the same, the circumstances are the same.** The major pitfalls described above, from pre/post analyses to comparisons of self-selected users and non-users, aren't applicable for experiments because the only thing that is different between the groups is whether they received the benefit or not.

Why don't vendors run experiments?

First and foremost, vendors don't supply experimental evidence of their program's impact because companies don't require them. It is up to HR departments to demand experimental data. Simple pre/post analyses are faster and often cheaper to provide than experiments; naturally, vendors will opt for a faster and cheaper route if they are given the choice.

Some vendors are not familiar with experimental techniques, and go with what they know. Again, prompting from HR departments can overcome this hurdle. In some cases, experiments are impractical — especially when very large samples are required or the programs address a problem that only occurs very rarely and can't be separately identified. However, in those cases, the program probably isn't worth the expense anyway. The larger an impact a program has, the smaller the sample size it needs. "Insufficient sample size" often simply means "not a big enough impact".[88]

Another, more subtle, reason why vendors and brokers don't provide experimental evidence is that they are already convinced that their program works. They look for evidence showing that "fact"; running an experiment would be like an admission of uncertainty. The more invested a person is in a program, the more time and energy they've put into developing it, the harder it can be to question its fundamental assumptions and value. Again, this isn't a problem that vendors are usually able to solve on their own — it takes a firm request from HR departments to drive change in the industry.

Matching techniques

When it isn't possible to compare the results of a program against a randomized selected control group, there is a second-best option that vendors can use. That is to "construct" a control group based on copious data about individuals, those who were offered the program and those who weren't.

Statistical matching aims to find people who weren't offered the program but who were otherwise identical to those who were offered it. You then compare outcomes for the constructed (matched) control group against outcomes for the people who were offered the benefit program. The challenge is that it can be very difficult to construct a truly identical control group, and impossible to prove that it has been done correctly.

In order to use this technique, vendors would have to have gathered detailed information about individuals who were not offered the program, and measured the outcomes of interest for them (retirement contributions, employee health, employee job satisfaction, etc.). The vendor would then use sophisticated statistical methods to construct the control group from the pool of people not

---

[88] There is one notable exception — and that's very noisy data. Noise in the data makes it harder to find the impact, even when it is there. However, that means it's harder to find using any statistically honest technique, and vendors and HR teams should consider the benefit program "inconclusive".

offered the program, and to ensure that two groups were identical. It can be done, but it is not a trivial process.

The outcomes must be measured the same way for both groups — which is difficult when measurement occurs *as part of the program itself,* like it does with many wellness providers. And, the "control" group can't be people who were offered the program but declined it — since by declining the program, they are illustrating how different they are than those who opt in!

Statistical matching is valuable because it provides an option when experiments truly aren't possible. However, there are many caveats that go with them. As noted above, they are difficult to execute correctly. And, with complexity comes the opportunity for being misled — intentionally and unintentionally.

Unique Outcomes

There's an important special case where statistical matching and randomized experiments aren't needed — and that is where the outcome the vendor measures, and that the employer cares about, is truly unique to the program. For example, let's say an employer is looking to offer an HSA and the only thing it cares about is whether or not people actually contribute to the HSA. That outcome — contributing to the HSA can't occur without the HSA. There's no need to run an experiment or statistical model to see the impact.

But, these situations aren't common. For example, often an employer will care about more than just sign-ups for HSAs — it will want to know if it causes people to save more for medical expenses (inside or outside of the HSA), because of the HSA. That requires an experiment.

Generating the Evidence You Need

Maybe the vendors you're talking with haven't gathered any experimental or statistically matched evidence of the impact of their programs. Again, most vendors will only do what's required of them by the market to sell their product, and that's normal. But, if you're asking, they should be willing to get those numbers — to win your business and to win business away from other vendors who don't supply hard impact numbers.

You can partner with your vendors to test the impact of a program. The easiest way to do that is with a **staggered rollout.**

> *A staggered rollout is a type of experiment in which everyone receives a new benefits offering, but it takes time to roll out the program.*

The key is that the people who receive it first are randomly selected.

Let's say you want to test a new wellness program, centering around yoga classes. You take all of the people who will be eligible for the yoga class and put their names in a list. You then randomly order the list and offer people at the top of the list about the class first. It can be the top 5%, top 20% or top 50% — it depends on a quick statistical test called a "power calculation" that the vendor can run using free, online tools. You email those people and let them sign up for the program.[89] Then, after the program *should* have had its impact,[90] you measure outcomes for the people who were invited versus those who weren't, and determine the program's impact.[91] *If things go well, you can roll out the program to everyone else.*

As you can see, a staggered rollout design is quite similar to the pilot programs that many companies already run — the difference lies in

---

[89] For anyone else who asks about the program, you can tell them that the program will be available shortly.

[90] There isn't a hard and fast rule for how long the delay should be between the initial rollout and measuring outcomes — it's however long the vendor says the program needs to work its magic.

[91] There are numerous variations on this theme, depending on the details of the program. For example, where measurement of the outcomes (like financial or physical wellness) is part of the program itself, then the vendor would a) roll out the program to the initial randomly selected group and b) roll it out to the others and then c) compare outcome on the day of the second set of rollouts across the two groups — the group that has had the program for a long time, and the group that just received it that day.

the initial randomization process. Staggered rollouts allow companies to field test a program before committing to a full purchase and making adjustments for a larger rollout, and they allow the company to accurately determine the causal impact at the same time. If the vendor is truly confident of its results, it will agree to be paid only if its program is shown to work — as a few companies like Omada Health[92] are currently doing.

Often, the company or its prospective vendors can recruit third-party academics to independently conduct the study and verify the results. Researchers know that experiments are the gold standard for evidence, and are often excited to work with companies that are willing to test programs in the real world. They help gather the information that companies need (usually for free), and receive a high-quality analysis for publication in return.[93]

A Quick Recap

❖ Make sure to ask vendors their *causal impact:* What is the change in *outcomes*, driven by observable changes in *employee behavior*, which is *caused by* the program?

❖ Unfortunately, most of the numbers provided by vendors, brokers, and benefits consultants aren't relevant or are misleading. Participant surveys are notoriously bad, but other common techniques — like comparing benefits offerings across an industry, pre/post analyses of participants, and comparisons of participants and non-participants — are similarly flawed.

❖ Focus on the metrics that the company really cares about and beware distractions. Often participation in a program just isn't that important; ask for evidence of the real impact that participation is supposed to engender.

---

[92] See "Price for Performance" at https://omadahealth.com/outcomes/

[93] Organizations such as Ideas42 (www.ideas42.org) help facilitate these research relationships. It's also something we've done extensively at HelloWallet with our academic advisory board (http://www.hellowallet.com/research/advisory-board/).

❖ There are three robust techniques to gather causal impact: randomized experiments, statistical matching, and unique outcomes. You don't need to be experts in these methods, but the vendors and brokers asking for your company's money should gain the necessary expertise. They usually won't supply this information without your prompting.

❖ If solid data about the impact of a program isn't available, it's not difficult to partner with a vendor to gather it. You can run a staggered rollout — a type of experiment that's like a pilot, but with randomization. If the program works, everyone gets access to it. If it doesn't, then only the initial study group receives it. Often your company or the vendor can partner with independent academics for free, to conduct the staggered rollout and verify the results.

7
TESTING ASSUMPTIONS: EARLY AND OFTEN

You've analyzed your employees' needs, and you've crafted an appropriate intervention. Next, you should put it out in the field and see how things go, right? Not necessarily. There's a much more cost-effective way to go about it. In short, the idea is to run increasingly sophisticated tests *as you craft the benefits package,* and before the implementation process.

A "Lean" Approach

The idea of rapid, iterative testing is common in the software-development world, and it's how we develop our financial wellness offering at HelloWallet. This approach is inspired by the Lean Startup methods of Eric Ries and Ash Maurya.[94] The approach is starting to make inroads in the HR world, but isn't widely used yet.[95]

---

[94] See Ries (2011) and Maurya (2012).

[95] See http://startuptucson.com/2013/turbo-charge-enterprise-human-resources-with-lean-startup/.
See also http://hr.toolbox.com/blogs/musing-on-preemployment-screening/4-pitfalls-to-lean-start-up-in-human-resources-55879 for some warnings on what happens if you apply Lean methods without recognizing the unique circumstances of an HR environment. Lean Startup methods are

Here's how it works. Once you have identified your benefits intervention:

1. Write out what needs to happen for it to work — both what you need to do, and what you're assuming other people (employees, vendors, CHRO, etc.) will do.

2. Identify which assumptions are the *riskiest.* I.e., which parts are the most likely to fail.

3. Test the riskiest assumptions — gathering data about whether each risk is real, and how to overcome it.

4. Repeat Steps 2-3 until the remaining risks are acceptable, or you've decided the intervention actually isn't a good idea.

For example, let's say you're investigating new wellness benefits.

1. **Write out what needs to happen.** You'll need to gain the buy-in of senior leadership, secure the budget, finalize the contract with the vendor, establish the benefit's incentives, and communicate it to employees, etc. You're also assuming employees will read the communication, want the benefit, sign up for it, and continue to use it over time.

2. **Identify the *riskiest* assumptions.** Getting employees to actually continue to use the benefit over time is a real challenge, but maybe it's straightforward to contract with the vendor, and get leadership buy-in.

3. **Test the assumptions.** Closely examine the vendor's data (described in Chapter 6) to determine what its usage is (not just their best case touted in marketing materials) and whether its data actually apply to your company's situation. Then, field test the "key innovation" of the benefit — do

---

themselves inspired by a Japanese manufacturing approach called "Lean" or "Kaizen"; that approach is more widely used in HR. See http://shrmstore.shrm.org/lean-hr-introducing-process-excellence-to-your-practice.html, http://results.wa.gov/what-we-do/apply-lean; http://hr.uiowa.edu/lean

your employees like public competitions, or incentive programs, or easy online portals, etc.?

Look for Behavioral Obstacles at Each Step

The basic process is straightforward — write out what needs to happen, figure out what's risky, and test it. Each step that's supposed to happen is a potential obstacle — a potential risk (thankfully most won't actually be risky!). The CREATE model, which we learned about in Chapter 2, is an easy way to determine whether those obstacles are real, and why. In short, at each step where someone takes action (for example, an employee opening an email), six problems can occur:

- ❖ **Cues**, or problems of attention
- ❖ **Reactions**, or problems of prior associations
- ❖ **Evaluations**, or problems of the costs and benefits
- ❖ **Ability**, or problems of a lack of resources, knowledge, or confidence
- ❖ **Timing,** or problems of procrastination or lack of urgency
- ❖ **Experience**, or problems caused by negative experiences the person has had using the program in the past.

By thinking through each one, you can judge which of these problems are real — and therefore need to be tested and potentially fixed. Sometimes, thinking through the CREATE model is just a thought-experiment, and sometimes you have solid data and insight from your employees to draw upon. It depends on where you are in the plan design and delivery process. Let's consider two scenarios.

Scenario 1: Implementing a new program

If you are getting ready to implement a new benefit program, look over each major interaction employees will have with the program, and use CREATE like a checklist. Does the employee have a strong enough cue to think about the action, is a strong negative reaction likely to occur, etc.?

For example, let's say the company is rolling out a new set of healthcare plans — including a traditional PPO plan, and a consumer-driven health plan. The first step that employees take would be to decide among the plans. Will employees be cued to learn about the options and select one that is right for them? I.e., above and beyond the moment when they complete their open enrolment information and are forced to give fleeting attention to it. What emotional reaction are they likely to have — is there a strong predisposition against CDHPs already? How are they likely to evaluate the costs and benefits to them (this is different than what the strictly financial costs and benefits are — it's how they will calculate it themselves and evaluate the evidence). And so forth.

If employees select a CDHP, the next action that employees might take would be to set up and save money in a HSA — the HR team should go through the same CREATE process for that step as well. Effectively, for each step that employees would take to move from inaction to action, the HR team would see if there are likely obstacles in the CREATE process.

Scenario 2: Crafting updates to an existing program.

If you are modifying an existing program, then you already have a wealth of direct feedback from employees to draw from. If a program has underperformed, you've probably already heard all about it from your employees!

In addition to workplace chatter, observe employees as they are interacting with the program — signing up, using it, talking with fellow employees — to get additional insight into where they struggle. Are they problems of insufficient attention (the Cue), insufficient urgency (Timing), inability to act (Ability), etc.? Finding obstacles, and the right interventions to overcome them, should then spur testing before it is implemented for the full population of employees.

What's a Test?

You may have noticed that "test" here has a particular meaning — it means testing an *assumption* that things will work out as you've planned. An assumption that, if wrong, means the benefits intervention won't succeed. Often those assumptions will be about the benefit offering itself: People will use it, it actually does what it is supposed to (it helps people save money, get healthier), etc.

Sometimes assumptions exist about less-obvious aspects of the benefit offering that are still crucial to its success. For example: Adding an incentive program won't *discourage* people from participating in other, non-incentivized benefits, or that the new health program can actually be rolled out in time to meet government requirements.

Testing assumptions is something HR practitioners already do, of course — if there's something that feels uncertain or risky about a new benefit offering, a good team will dig into the details and figure out how to fix the problem. Here, we're simply looking at a more formalized, structured way of going about this process. By approaching the early testing process systematically, we can identify risks early, and "fail fast".

Failing Fast

It's important to test before implementing major changes to plan designs or communications because we all get things wrong. We accidently mistype something in a benefits email, which makes it laughable. We forget to include the date of a wellness event, and no one shows up. Or, more subtly, we have the wrong match-ratio of our 401(k) or HSA and end up costing the company millions of dollars without helping our employees.

Unfortunately, we can't avoid such mistakes altogether. However, we can find them *earlier* — before they are costly, embarrassing, or irreversible. Designers and engineers have a term for this idea, attributed to IDEO founder David Kelly: "Fail fast, succeed sooner"[96]

Some Examples

To make things more concrete, let's run through some example scenarios, in which an early test can help the HR team be more successful and cost-effective with its benefits offerings.

1. **Intervention:** Add a new voluntary benefit, like pet insurance.
   Risk identified: Will employees actually use it?
   Test: Find employees whose spouses already have the benefit. Did they elect to use the pet insurance?[97]

2. **Intervention:** Change the plate sizes in the company's cafeterias to help decrease portion sizes.
   Risk Identified: Angry employees.
   Test: One day, in one of the company's cafeterias, try placing smaller plates in front of the larger plates, to see if people actually care.

Here's a risk that many HR practitioners already account for, but may not think about as an explicit assumption to be tested:

3. **Intervention:** Increase the match rate for employees on their HSAs.
   Risk Identified: Exceeding the budget for HSA match dollars.
   Test: Look up the behavioral research on match rates, and how much they affect employee contributions (smaller than economic theory would predict).[98] Then run a few scenarios in Excel and

---

[96] E.g. http://csi.gsb.stanford.edu/fail-faster-succeed-sooner

[97] This is a good case in which surveys are a great, accurate tool. Instead of asking employees if they *want* pet insurance (knowing that employees often say yes, but don't follow through), ask them if they *do* use pet insurance. We're much better at answering about current behavior than about future desires and behavior.

[98] See Madrian (2012): assuming someone is already participating, match rates don't affect contributions much. In other studies of IRAs, increasing

see if new employee contribution rates are likely to cost too much in matching funds.

But, for the same type of intervention, other risks may be untested For example:

4. **Intervention:** Increase the match rate for employees on their HSAs.

   Risk Identified: Changing the match rate may not change participation rates much (based on behavioral research already in the field).

   Test: First, look at the company's prior experience with match rates on their 401(k). Has it ever changed the rate, and, if so, what happened? Second, put the question to employees. Ask them how much they would contribute if the HSA had the current rate versus the new proposed rate.[99]

Testing isn't (necessarily) a pilot project

In the HR world, when you talk about "testing before implementing", many people think of pilot projects. I.e., running a program in a few company locations and then rolling it out to the full employee population if all goes well. As the examples above show, that's only one type of test, and often not what's required.

To understand why, we need to consider the difference between *testing a risky aspect* of an intervention and *implementing a small intervention that's a bit risky*.

❖ *Testing a risky aspect of an intervention* means identifying the main risk and only testing that. For example, if you're not

---

the match rate significantly increase *participation*, especially among low income populations (Duflo et al. 2005)

[99] You'll need to be a bit creative in how you ask this question, though, to avoid employees comparing different rates and rationalizing that the higher rate means they should answer "contribute more". One way to do this, is to ask two sets of employees — one set gets the current rate (to see how different their answers are from what employees are *actually* contributing), and another set gets the proposed rate.

sure whether employees will actually use a voluntary benefit, you can talk with them first and see if they already pay for similar benefits on their own, before even searching for vendors who offer it.

❖ *Implementing a small, risky intervention* means going through the full process of implementing an intervention, both the risky aspects and the non-risky aspects. For example, if you're not sure about usage of a voluntary benefit across the company, you might offer it to employees in one division of the company. That is: Run a pilot project.

The problem with pilot projects is that they may require the HR team to put in almost the same work and effort as a full rollout. They can save the company money and embarrassment of rolling out a failed offering, which is valuable; but they still require significant overhead in getting leadership buy-in, contracting with a vendor, developing the communications, evaluating the program's effectiveness, etc. A wisely targeted test focuses on *only* the part that's most likely to cause problems. It requires the smallest amount of HR time and energy that's possible to understand the particular risk.

You can tell if you have a well-targeted (efficient) test, by asking:

❖ What risk does this test isolate and help us understand?

❖ Are we doing only what is *required* to test that risk?

A Quick Recap

❖ Testing before implementation can significantly decrease risks of a failed benefits rollout. The goal is to *fail fast* — to find the inevitable problems early, before they cause expensive (and embarrassing) problems with your company's benefits.

❖ Pre-implementation testing is straightforward.

    o Write out what you're assuming will happen with the intervention, especially what you're assuming others will do.

○ Identify the riskiest assumptions — those that are most likely to cause problems or not bear out.

○ Test those assumptions — by gathering more data to assess if the risk is real, and trying out ways to overcome those risks.

❖ You can use the CREATE funnel from Chapter 2 to see whether there are hidden and risky assumptions.

❖ Testing risky assumptions often doesn't mean running a pilot program — pilot programs may require all the work (but not all of the budget) of a full implementation. Properly targeted tests require only the minimum amount of work needed to test a risky assumption.

8

VALUING BENEFITS COMMUNICATIONS

Would you rather read this:

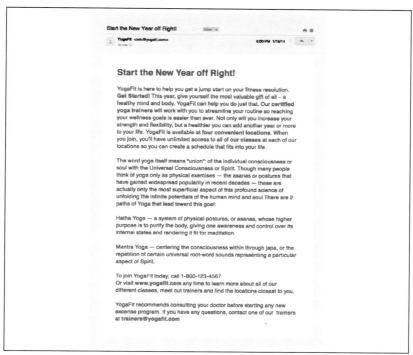

Figure 11: An all too common layout for employee communications

Or this:

Figure 12: Same content, just easier to read

If we don't want to read the first one ourselves, how can we blame our employees if they don't read and act on benefits communications that look like that? We've all seen communications that are like Big Lumps Of Text (or BLOTs, for short) from previous employers. Sometimes we've just ignored them; at other times, we've slogged through them but felt the effort along the way.

This chapter is the first of three chapters that focus on *implementing* benefits interventions. A key part of the implementation process is communicating new programs, and changes in existing ones, to employees. Yet, the art and science of effective communication isn't given the attention and value that it deserves. So, this chapter is about the importance of benefits communications broadly — and about a particular approach to communications, experimental optimization, that can greatly increase their effectiveness.

The next chapter provides a slew of behavioral techniques that can help improve the uptake and usage of a benefit program — through better benefits communications and more. Finally, the last chapter in the set, Chapter 10, provides tips and techniques you can use specifically when emailing your employees — something most of us do quite a lot of!

Let's start by singing the praises of benefits communication — something we all should do more of.

Communication Drives Action

Surprisingly, benefits communications is given relatively little attention in the HR literature. For example, in the 842-page *WorldAtWork Handbook on Total Rewards*, only one out of 24 chapters is about benefits communications, and only *two* pages actually give guidance on the content of employee communications. A survey by Benz Communications showed that only a tiny portion of benefits spending goes to communication.[100] Moreover, while there are numerous injunctions in HR about the importance of "communicating effectively",[101] there's surprisingly little guidance available about the details of what that means and how, exactly, one should be communicating.

I believe that the relative lack of attention comes from a misunderstanding: *That benefits communication is about information.* As WorldAtWork defines it, "communication can be...defined as creating understanding and transferring meaning."[102]

---

[100] Benz (2012)

[101] e.g. Foster et al. (2012)

[102] WorldAtWork (2007)

Communicating information is straightforward — tell people what they need to know, and what's legally required. Practitioners really shouldn't need more guidance, right? Thus, it should be no surprise that practitioners say, "I've told them what they need to know" and leave it at that. It's similarly natural to give little attention to communications because that should be the vendor's job. Or, to not invest in communications because of restrictions from compliance on content. But communication is exactly where we need to invest to improve the impact of benefits. Communication can't be left (only) to vendors, and can't only include legally required language.

The problem is that information (understanding and meaning) is just one part of the puzzle, and often the *least* important part of it. Instead, HR communications are a means to trigger employee action — action that helps employees, the employer, or, hopefully, both. *Telling* employees about their new wellness program is good; but if that communication doesn't spur those who need and would like the program to actually *use* it, what's the point of sending out the communication in the first place? Even messages that appear to be purely informational — telling people about new contribution limits for their 401(k)s or HSAs, have value to the employee *because of the action they drive*. For example, for people who are contributing up to the old contribution limit, the messages triggers employees to raise contributions up to the new limit. HR has the power to support action, not just inform.

Benefits communications are where the rubber hits the road in the behavioral approach to benefits — they cue employees to think about action, generate an emotional response (and all too often, an intuitive negative reaction that stops them from proceeding further), convey costs and benefits, and help employees determine if they have the ability and the right timing to act. The plan design process sets up the right inputs, but it's the communication itself that CREATEs action.

Putting that knowledge into practice

So, what does this realization — communications drive action — practically mean for benefits communications?

120

1. For any communication, make sure the action it seeks to drive is clear. If you don't know what you're asking employees to do, neither will they.

2. Look for obstacles to CREATE Action — is the communication likely to get employees' attention? Will employees have a positive reaction? Will they know the costs and benefits? The communication should help employees overcome those obstacles

3. Test assumptions. Any communication can be improved, and that we'll always get some things wrong. But, if we carefully test our assumptions — as early as possible — we can create more powerful communications and avoid embarrassing mistakes.

This should sound very familiar — we've covered all of this already in the book. In fact, we replicate the overall process of creating effective *benefits* when we create effective *communications* about those benefits. With benefit communications, though, there are unique opportunities that HR teams can take advantage of. The next two chapters cover techniques you can use to overcome CREATE obstacles. There's also an opportunity to test assumptions and improve their impact — via experimental optimization.

Experimental Optimization

Every time we roll out a benefits intervention — whether it is a new benefit program, a change to an existing one, or a new communication with employees about their benefits — there are opportunities to test and learn for the future. In most cases, that testing process is informal: The benefits intervention goes out to employees, and we watch what happens. We then apply those lessons to later rollouts, at some point in the future.

We can learn faster — and develop more effective communications — by changing that rollout process. Instead of rolling out an intervention to everyone all at once, we can do a staggered rollout — in which employees receive the intervention in waves over time. For example, one-third of the employees can receive it in the first week;

the second third the next week, and the final third the week after that.

I briefly covered the mechanics of staggered rollouts in Chapter 6, and how they can be used to evaluate the true impact of a vendor's offering. Here, it's the same mechanics, but for a different purpose — to test assumptions, learn as you go along, and not have to wait for the "next time".

That may be a bit too abstract, so let's go through an example. This process works especially well for optimizing the uptake and usage of your benefits via benefits communications, so let's look at that domain.

An Example: Optimizing Communications Around a New Benefit

Let's say your company is making HSA accounts available to employees. You've identified the core risk (employees not understanding what the HSA is) and you've developed some good information to overcome it. But, there's disagreement on the team on exactly how the email that conveys that information should look. One group says it should be plain text, just the facts. Another says it should be full of pictures and styled HTML to make it more visually interesting.

So, instead of arguing, you can test it. You'll send out the email in two waves. In the first wave, you'll send out *both* versions of the email to two different groups of employees; in the second wave you'll send the "winning" email to everyone else. That way, you can learn what works, and make sure that most employees get the best email.

To put some numbers around this, imagine that one of the emails really appeals to people: 20% of people sign up for the HSA. The other emails don't, and only 10% sign up (variations like that are actually quite common with email). The problem is that you don't know which one will work best — the team is arguing. If you don't optimize, you can expect either 10% or 20% to sign up. A big difference, and a big risk. If you do optimize, using one-quarter of the employees in the first wave, you are certain to get 19% of employees signing up, with no risk. You, your employees, and your health plan, are much better off. [103]

How the Process Works

Stepping back from this example, the team would do six things to optimize its benefit communications:

1. **Identify communication risks**. After you've done your pre-rollout testing, figure out where you still see big risks, or where you see great opportunities for improvement.

2. **Generate multiple approaches** to handle those risks or take advantage of those opportunities.

3. **Determine how many employees you need.** to tell if one version if better than another. If you are running a formal experiment, described in Chapter 6, then you use an online calculator to quickly tell you how many employees are needed.

4. **Randomly select that number of employees** (or job sites) into two groups. That way, you can focus on just the impact of the two communications, and not on other differences that might exist between the two groups of recipients (Chapter 6 describes the logic of random assignment in more detail).

5. **Test the two versions.** That is, send the communication to the two randomly selected groups, see who takes action most frequently (i.e., signs up for the wellness program, or changes their retirement contributions, etc.)

---

[103] If you don't test, you have a 50% probability of the picking the "good" email, with 20% uptake, and a 50% probability of the picking the "bad" email, with 10% uptake. If you do test, and you have sufficient sample size to accurately tell which email is "good" based on your test, then in the first wave you have 12.5% of the population receiving the "good" email, and 12.5% receiving the "bad" email, and you figure out which one is good and which one is bad. In the second wave, all 75% remaining employees receive the good email. The result is an expected uptake of 18.75%. Good job!

6. **Send the winner to everyone else.** Everyone you didn't send the test emails to gets the benefit of your learning from the first round.

Let's look at another example. The HR team notices that employees aren't using the FSA program, despite its tax benefits, and wants to send an email to employees encouraging them to use it. You identify a key risk: how the email talks about the FSA's "use it or lose it" rule. You generate two versions of the email: One version tackles the issue head on, and draws employee attention to it. The doesn't make a big issue of the "use it or lose it" rule, and just links to the IRS site for more information for those are curious. You determine how many employees you need; out of a population of 10,000 employees, you'll need 500 employees to receive each version of the email, or 1,000 total.

You then randomly place 500 employees into each group. You take the list of employees in Excel, generate two new columns. One just has the word "=Rand()" for each employee (to generate a random number), and the other uses the "Index()" function (to select employees into Group 1 or Group 2); you can look at sites like http://www.extendoffice.com/documents/excel/645-excel-select-cells-randomly.html for an example of how to do it.

You then send out the email and determine that it's best to tackle the FSA issue head on. 35% of employees took action on that one, and only 15% did with the other FSA email. You apply this lesson to the rest of the population. Because of this simple test, an additional 9% of our employees will benefit from the FSA.[104]

And that's it. You can learn what works best, and ensure that most employees get the best version (instead of guessing which one is best), just by rolling it out to employees over time and learning from the first wave of the rollout.

---

[104] Without the test, you'll get either 35% or 15% of employees, with an assumed equal likelihood. That's 2,500 employees or 25% in expectation. With the test you have (35%*500 + 15%*500) employees in the first round, and (35%*9000) employees in the second round, or 34% of employees. 34%-25%=9%.

Multiple Iterations

In fact, you don't need to stop with only one round of optimization. You can keep iterating on Steps 1-6 for as many different aspects of the communication as you'd like, until you've communicated with all of your employees. Each round of optimization, the communication gets better and better, and employees are better off.

For example, let's say you have 10,000 employees, and for each optimization, you need 1,000 employees to tell which one is best. You could actually optimize in 10 different areas, learning and applying each time. If you're sending the FSA email described above, you can optimize who sends the message, what it looks like, what it says, when you send it, etc., all in the same rollout. The result is a polished, tested, highly effective communication that increases the usage of the benefit manifold — all in the span of a single rollout.

Experimental Optimization at HelloWallet

Experimental optimization is one of the most enjoyable and rewarding parts of my work at HelloWallet, and it's something that we're well known for in the field. For example, with a single company, we ran more than 80 tests in a six-week period. We tested who should send the message, the subject line, the time of day, the formatting of the message, the basic description of the program — even the color of the buttons.

In total, those tests *doubled the uptake of the program,* despite the fact that we started the new testing process with a well-designed set of communications that we had tested and honed over numerous previous engagements. And, an impact that large isn't unusual. We ran another series of tests that focused on usage of the program — similarly *doubling* usage over a three-month period.

What Experimental Optimization Doesn't Mean

When working with benefits teams on experimental optimization, they naturally have questions about how it works in practice. Here are some of the most common questions I've encountered:

Will employees get conflicting messages?

When you are optimizing communications — telling employees about a benefit, for example — each employee receives one and only one message. Different (randomly selected) groups of employees receive different messages, at least in the initial waves.

Won't some employees get a "bad" version?

By optimizing your communications, you *discover* that one version is better than others. You don't send a bad version more often than you would have otherwise — you simply learn which of your communications should be improved!

In fact, you significantly and verifiably *decrease* the number of employees who receive less optimal versions through experimental optimization. In a simple example, let's say you have two equally viable options for everything — two incentive formulas, two vendors, two benefits communications, etc. If you don't optimize, on average, employees will receive "bad" versions 50% of the time. If you do optimize, employees will receive "bad" versions far less; from 25% to 1% of the time, depending on how you structure the optimization.

Isn't this a lot of extra work?

Optimizing doesn't require much additional time and effort beyond tracking whether the rollout is successful — i.e., beyond what the HR team or vendor should be doing anyway. It builds on the fact that you (should) know, per employee, whether they are signed up for and are using a benefit program. It also builds on staggered rollouts — which, as we discussed in Chapter 6, are the primary way you can assess how much a benefit program is actually helping your employees.

Experimental Optimization of Plan design

Thus far, we've intentionally focused on how you can optimize uptake and usage of a program through benefit communications. But, it's worth noting that you may be able to optimize the core design of the benefit itself, especially when the current design has run into problems. We'll take a brief detour from the topic of benefit communications to explore an example, optimizing the usage of a wellness benefit.

Let's say you work in a large company with many job sites scattered across the country. The company has a wellness program that hasn't worked out well — very few people are using it regularly. You're not sure how to get people excited about it, though. You have a few different options that have passed your initial feedback gathering and testing with employees. One option is to incentivize employees — basically, pay them to participate. Another option is to do a competition — publicize the most active person, give them a prize etc. Both seem reasonable, but your company doesn't have the budget do so both. So, you iteratively try them out — with a few job sites, you do direct incentives. With a few other job sites, you do a competition. You see what happens with the usage of the wellness program. Then, you take what you've learned, and use the best program across the rest of the job sites.

In this case, if you *don't* optimize, you're taking a very significant risk. You could waste your company's incentive money, fail to increase usage of the wellness program, or both. If you *do* optimize, you're certain that you'll have the best option for the majority of your employees.

Special Opportunities and Challenges

As you're planning out, and testing, your benefits communications, there is one factor to pay particular attention to — timing. When it comes to employees using their benefits, most days are like all the others, but a few are truly unique and provide an opportunity for making major decisions and changing daily routines.

Remember from Chapter 2 that much of our daily behavior is controlled by nonconscious processes, like habits. Every day, what types of food we will eat, how we will go to work, how we will interact with our colleagues and boss, and what we will spend money on — all of these are largely decided before we wake up in the morning. The times when that *isn't* the case are surprisingly few.

Throughout this book, we discuss ways to grab employee attention away from their everyday routine — with benefits communications, with competitions, with incentive programs, etc. There are two other options, however, that take a different approach

1. Look for times when employees are already thinking about their benefits directly, or the part of their lives that the benefit affects, and build on that attention to ask them to make key decisions. For example, employees come to expect open enrollment, and even though they may not devote as much time as they should to those choices, they do think about their benefits then. Similarly, when parents are paying their dependent care bills, they are likely already thinking about ways to pay less money (like FSAs).

2. Focus on the times when routines are already disrupted. When employees are starting a new job, moving to a new job site, or changing roles within their job, their routines at work at in flux (or unformed). At these times, it's possible to start employees down a path of healthier eating, exercise, spending money differently, etc. Similarly, when employees are going through a major life transition *outside* of work — marriage, divorce, the birth of a new child — those are times when existing routines are disrupted and new routines are formed.

These two options seek to align with employee attention, instead of trying to change where employees put their attention. Aligning with moments of attention is more subtle, and uses forethought and planning instead of brute force.

A Quick Recap

❖ Benefits communications are about action, not just information. Communications are the HR team's primary tool to cue employees to decide on their benefits elections, set their contributions, and follow through on wellness program commitments. Without effective communications, a wonderfully designed program usually fails.[105]

❖ To improve benefits communications, we can employ the same tools we've discussed throughout this book to make the benefits themselves more effective — setting clear goals, identifying obstacles to action, prioritizing risks, and testing assumptions.

❖ Experimental Optimization is a powerful tool that HR teams can use to test assumptions and increase the impact of their benefits communications. Here's how it works:

  o When you are ready to communicate with employees about a new benefit program or a change to an existing one, identify the open questions and opportunities — such as novel ideas that the HR team has to improve the uptake or usage of the benefit.

  o Determine how many employees you need to see which version of the communication is best (when you test with a randomized experiment, there are easy online calculations)

  o Implement the two versions of the communication with only that subset of people. Measure which version was the best.

---

[105] 401(k) auto-enrollment is a partial exception — in which employees aren't expected to take action. But, as we've discussed earlier, auto-enrollment without employee buy-in leads to numerous problems downstream — plan leakage, tax penalties, etc.

o Send the winning communication to the rest of the employees.

❖ At HelloWallet, we've regularly found that one can *double* the uptake and usage of a benefit through experimental optimization.

9
IMPLEMENTING FOR
UPTAKE AND USAGE

You've evaluated the evidence, designed an excellent benefit program, and made sure it's what employees and the company needs.

At some point, you'll hit a challenge though: How do you ensure that the employees who really need and want the program actually benefit from it? No matter what the program is, it really doesn't matter whether the company has it or not, if no one uses it.[106] In this chapter, we'll talk about how to apply specific targeted techniques from the behavioral literature to help employees bridge the gap between intending to use a benefit, and actually doing so. We'll build on the six strategic types of benefits interventions available to employers, which we discussed in Chapter 5, and add numerous additional options.

---

[106] Unless the program is only for sexy promotional material for job candidates, but aren't actually used by anyone. That's a bad strategy though; if a prospect joins the company and finds that the program isn't what it's cracked up to be, then there will suddenly be a retention problem!

Setting the Stage

The tactics discussed here assume that the team has already accomplished four things.

1. Analyzed the needs of employees and the employer to determine what outcomes and specific actions (or behaviors) are being targeted. *See Chapter 4.*

2. Crafted the strategic benefits intervention — a change in the lineup, a change in the financial incentives, a new promotion campaign, etc. *See Chapter 5.*

3. If the team is making a change in the lineup, they have carefully evaluated the evidence for the new program. *See Chapter 6.*

4. Designed the core financial incentives to ensure that the program is, in fact, a "benefit" — i.e., in the financial interest of employees, and better than what they can get on the open market.

5. Identified and tested these riskiest assumptions about the intervention (except, perhaps, "employees will use it"; we'll help with that here). *See Chapter 7.*

If these pieces are in place, HR professionals can still hit the common scenario: a well-designed, valuable, employee-requested benefit that isn't actually used.

How to improve uptake and usage

Cues: Problems of Attention

As discussed in Chapter 2, few employees are going to sign up for a program if they simply aren't aware of it. Thankfully, this is a relatively easy problem for employers to solve.

It requires a concrete and pragmatic view of employee attention. Look for channels of communication that already have employee attention, and hook into them. If employees aren't reading benefits posters or the details of their open enrollment packages — then don't belabor them (at least not in their current form). If they aren't opening emails from HR, don't expect people to change. Instead, change tactics:

Solution 1: Move in front of the employee's eye. If an email from the benefits team isn't getting employee attention, consider: What *are* employees paying attention to? Is there is a timekeeping website that employees regularly use to log their hours, and is it possible to reach employees there? If the employees are frequent SMS users, do corporate policy allow you to *try* sending text messages to a small group of employees? If employees frequently use social media, and are already connected to an employer-controlled account, then try getting employee attention there. [107] Above all — are there in-person, 1:1 meetings with HR staff who could quickly draw employee attention to the program? Each of these tactics involves changing the attention-getting route, and not changing where employees put their attention. [108]

However, this doesn't mean you can simply switch channels — sending out the same content as before via a new, more powerful channel. If the prior content bored or discouraged employees, they'll quickly learn to tune out the content in a new channel, too. That's why cueing isn't enough — the team must plan out the interaction to ensure that strong negative reactions (like "Ugh. Boring …") are avoided, the costs and benefits make sense, etc.. — i.e., that other obstacles don't occur further down the line that ruin the impact of the cue.

---

[107] The fact that employees use social media isn't enough on its own. If they aren't paying attention to the employer's social media accounts, then you are back at square one. You may *also* want to improve the quality and value of the social media account, to win over employees in the long term, but that is another task altogether.

[108] It seems wrong, doesn't it? Shouldn't we find ways to "make" employees pay attention? Emphatically No. To increase the usage of a program, we need to adapt to the realities of employees, rather than trying to force them to adapt to the program.

Solution 2: Highlight the single next step that's needed. When we cue employees about their benefits, we want to ensure that we're cueing them to take action immediately and in some meaningful way, and not asking them to wade through a pile of materials, learn everything about the benefit, and then figure out what to do next.

We don't want them to guess what to do, or start off by making complex choices about which next step is really right for them. This isn't about avoiding the real work — it's about making sure that the path to act is clear. Remember that the cue to act triggers an immediate emotional reaction — if it looks confusing or difficult, people will postpone it. Thus the cue itself — the action we're asking people to take — sets the stage for that reaction.

In Chapter 10, we'll talk in detail about how to structure the "Call to Action", as the cue is known in email marketing. But in general, these simple guidelines can help: Ask employees to do one thing at a time, make the ask upfront (don't bury it at the bottom of a poster, for example), and express exactly what employees will be doing as clearly as possible (instead of "start the sign up process", "get your free gym membership").

Solution 3: Try again. Behavioral researchers have found how remarkably effective a simple reminder can be for motivating action. Simply put — employees are busy people. We may be too busy to really think about a program when we're first asked about it, or we may forget the things we'd planned to do. There's nothing wrong with reminding people about an action that's needed on their benefits — as long as it's done without implying that employees are lazy or disinterested. How busy we are ebbs and flows over time, and so it's important to try contacting employees at different times of day or days of the week with each reminder.

Reaction: Problems of Prior Association

Solution 1: Social Proof (Show that it's normal). Some employees don't use a program because it's unfamiliar, and that naturally makes people uncomfortable. One powerful way to overcome that sense of unease is to show that their colleagues are already using the program.

The technique is known as social proof, that's what Facebook is doing with its "Likes" counter on a post. Facebook is showing the reader that other readers (their friends) already "like" it, and so should the reader.

Solution 2: Personalization. Like it or not, some employees have a strong negative reaction to the faceless entity "HR". If an actual person, especially someone they know, asks them to use their benefits, that makes the call to action much more personal and powerful. Behavioral researchers have studied the impact of personal versus impersonal requests, and found that in general, we all respond much better to actual human beings!

Solution 3: Beautiful design. It may seem strange in a book about behavioral research, but beauty matters. As we discussed in Chapter 2, a beautiful design can help employees sidestep existing associations they have about "boring benefits communications". In addition, if a benefit program is presented in an aesthetically pleasing way, *especially the actual poster, email, or web page that asks them to sign up for it,* people are more likely to respond positively. If we like something in one area, like its outward appearance, we tend to like it in other areas as well (what researchers call the "halo effect").

Our intuitive reactions really are about judging a book by its cover — and so it behooves the HR team to ensure that the cover is beautiful. This is a common focus of study in the design field. Similarly, researchers have found that our sense of trust also builds upon our assessments of how professional a site looks. [109]

Evaluation: Problems of Costs and Benefits

Employees may want to use a program, but are unsure of the exact costs and benefits, or feel the net value to them isn't sufficiently high. In that case, there are a few routes to pursue — assuming that the program really is in the employee's best interest.

---

[109] See Anderson (2011) for examples of psychology in design — particularly the effective of beauty. See for example Fogg et al. (2001) on trust and professional design.

Solution 1: Highlight the most relevant benefits. We're just not that good at making compound value judgments across multiple criteria at once. Instead, we tend to use our prior experience and simplifying heuristics to quickly assess whether something is generally worthwhile or not.

In a benefits context, however, we often directly ask employees to make complex judgments without the benefit of prior experience or accurate rules of thumb for what to do. What can we do about that? We can focus attention on the benefits that are most relevant to employees.

Remember that *financial* benefits may not be the most relevant. In fact, highlighting the lower cost of a program may turn people off, if they see it as a sign of lower quality. As Charles DeSantis, Chief Benefits Officer at Georgetown University put it nicely with respect to their health insurance offerings "But people respond weirdly to a lesser priced product."

Solution 1b: If it's free for the employee, say that loud and clear

While people respond oddly to low-priced products, nothing beats the joy of getting something valuable for free. Dan Ariely, in his book *Predictably Irrational*, describes a series of tests he ran in which products (like chocolates) were priced at 1 cent or free — the simple label "free" caused a stampede of desire for the free product, where pricing them at 1 cent didn't.

In fact, in one of our experiments at HelloWallet, we unintentionally documented the impact of "free" with our financial wellness software. We were testing social proof (see "reaction") and accidentally dropped the word "free" from the header of one of our emails: and saw an immediate 35% drop in enrollments.

Solution 2: Make it a competition. Competitions effectively change the types of costs and benefits that we think about. Instead of looking at the purely financial aspects, they focus us on social returns — having fun with friends, not looking like a loser in front of our colleagues, doing our duty to support our team.

Solution 3: Show them what they'll lose (Loss aversion). People respond much more strongly to losses than to gains. Researchers have found that people are often be willing to forfeit twice as much money to keep an item that they already have, than they are willing to pay to purchase an otherwise identical item.[110]

These lessons can readily be applied to benefits communications. Instead of touting the money gained, HR teams can highlight how much employees will *lose* in matching employer contributions if they under-contribute to their HSA or 401(k)s. The math is exactly the same, but the psychology is not.

However, loss aversion is, by definition, negative. It should be used sparingly and always tested to ensure that it does not backfire. Employees may tune out or get upset at HR communications that are consistently negative. Loss aversion is a technique that's risky, but also very powerful.

Ability: Problems of Resources or Confidence

Solution 1: Make it easier

If employees put off using their benefits because of some step they have to take along the way, *remove or simplify that step*. This extends a lesson from Chapter 5 — use automation and defaults where possible, and simplification where not. For example, if employees are failing to go to a centralized weigh-in station at the end of each week during a weight-loss program, make it easier to weigh-in — with decentralized stations or Internet-enabled scales that submit the information automatically. Omada Health follows this route, for example.[111]

Another, related way to make the task easier is to break it into smaller pieces, so that the immediate next step is much more manageable. Then, as the employee takes each smaller step, give positive feedback — celebrate small wins as they are made[112] For example, preparing for major medical expenses is potentially

---

[110] For example, Kahneman and Tversky (1984)

[111] Sepah (2014).

[112] "Small wins" refers to the surprising joy and boost people get from seemingly minor successes. See Amabile and Kramer (2011).

overwhelming task; and one where many employees would not know where to start. The HR team can instead present employees with the specific, small steps on that path, such as: Go to the company's site, go to the specific page with total claims paid for last year, go to the company's HSA provider site, etc.

Solution 2: Decrease the number of options

Everyone, employees included, can become overwhelmed when confronted with choices that have too many options — especially when the options are not directly comparable on a single dimension.

If you *ask* employees if they would like more health insurance options, or more retirement plan options, they will generally say yes. Yet, when actually confronted with the choice among such options, researchers have found that people suffer choice overload — avoiding the decision altogether, procrastinating, or making a poor, heuristic based choice instead of carefully evaluating the best course of action.

This situation is known as the "paradox of choice". It has been documented in such diverse areas as 401(k) plans, prescription drug coverage, and buying jam at a supermarket.[113]

The solution is straightforward — decrease the number of options *presented at one time*. That may mean decreasing the number of options overall, or it may mean creating a hierarchical or sequential display, so people can manage a smaller choice set at once.

Solution 3: Elicit Implementation Intentions

Sometimes people fully intend to do something, start at it, then run into an obstacle and get distracted. That obstacle may be small and easy to overcome — like when employees plan to fill out an enrollment form on the benefits portal, but hit a question asking for

---

[113] "401(k) plans:" Iyengar et al. (2003); "Prescription drug coverage:" Hanoch et al. (2009); "Jam at a supermarket:" Iyengar and Lepper (2000). Like most interesting results, this one is not without controversy. See Scheibehenne et al. (2010) for a summary of studies in the field and Thompson (2013) for a popular-press overview. From an HR practitioner perspective, there's a simple response to the scholarly disagreement — if you see people struggle with lots of options, try decreasing them.

an employee ID number they don't know offhand. *Implementation intentions* are one way to help employees overcome these obstacles.

Implementation intentions are specific plans that people make on how to act in the future[114]; they tell the mind to do X whenever Y happens. Here's how it works: You ask employees to write out *how* they will do something in the future — like going to the gym. When will they go? What clothes will they bring? Who will take care of the kids? What will they do if it's raining? Etc. [115] By thinking through *now* what the employee needs to do *later,* that can help the employee both anticipate future obstacles, and, when an obstacle does occur, have a plan of action ready to go without stopping to think about it and getting distracted.

Timing: Problems of Urgency and Procrastination

Solution 1: Accept Temporal Myopia & Focus on the Present

Remember that humans are hard-wired to think about the present, and excessively discount future gains — what behavioral economists call "temporal myopia"?[116] Unfortunately, some benefits provide value to employees *only* in the future — like HSAs and FSAs which help at tax time and 401(k)s which help at retirement. In the near term, to be frank, they require upfront pain and little reward. That's a recipe for procrastination.

Instead of exhorting employees to think about the future, there's an easier option — ask them to think about the present. Look for the value that a benefit program provides *now* instead of in the future. That value can be financial, like "every time you deposit to your 401(k) you'll *immediately* receive matching funds from the company". The value can also be social — like the examples of social proof or

---

[114] See Gollwitzer (1999) on implementation intentions.

[115] You don't need to ask these personal details directly, of course. Instead, you ask them to plan it out, and give questions like these as an example.

[116] See Chapter 2, where we introduced the idea of temporal myopia.

competitions mentioned above — as long as the HR team highlights that it's *immediate* and not something far off in the future.

Solution 2: Use Incentives & Scarcity

One way to show employees that there is value in a benefit program now is to use incentives — either with cash or a "chance to win" a prize, like an iPad.[117] Provide a deadline by which employees need to take action to receive the incentive (or chance to win the prize); that creates urgency, as long as the incentive is valuable enough.

Another, related way to layer on immediacy and urgency is to employ scarcity. I.e., you can provide a prize for the first set of people who take action. Offer cash or a sweepstakes for the first 100 people who sign up for the new wellness program, for example. The incentive is completely unrelated to the long-term benefits of the wellness program, but it may be enough to get employees in the door, with the expectation that the program itself is interesting enough to keep them engaged afterwards.

There's a major downside to these approaches through — once the limited-time or limited-quantity incentive is gone, people who missed out may be *less* motivated than if there hadn't been an incentive at all. So, it's a calculation of risk: Does the incentive provide enough urgency to encourage people to *start* the action, and is the program itself interesting enough to keep them without continued incentives, that it outweighs the risk of turning off those who aren't included?[118]

Solution 3: Use Focal Dates and Deadlines

When something is always important but never urgent, the HR team can help employees take action by providing a *specific day and time* to

---

[117] You may be asking why we *didn't* discuss incentives in the last section — the evaluation of costs and benefits. That's because we're looking at programs that are true "benefits" — they are in the interest of the employee, and the benefits should already outweigh the costs. Additional incentives however can provide urgency when lacking.

[118] The limited incentive program can also kick-start the social community that supports a benefit as well. If it gets enough people using the benefit, and talking about it, that can help create the social proof (see "Reaction" section) that encourages other people to join as well.

do it. The most obvious case is a deadline — telling employees that they need to complete a particular form by a certain date (even without offering an additional incentive or prize for doing so). Open enrollment periods are effectively simultaneous deadlines for actions that otherwise wouldn't otherwise be urgent — adjusting one's health plan, changing retirement contribution levels, etc.

However, deadlines aren't the only answer; other, more gentle and friendly approaches can still be effective. One option is to use specificity — just ask employees to take action on a *particular* day. An example I use frequently at HelloWallet is this:

"John, you should really review your retirement contribution."

"John, on Thursday night, at 9 p.m., you should talk with your spouse in the dining room and review your retirement contribution."

The latter feels more real, more motivating, simply because it is more specific. It's one of the many quirks of our minds.

Another option is to create an event around the action, and encourage people to all participate at once. Charles DeSantis at Georgetown University employs a great example of this — the 12:30 Thursday walk.

Figure 13: The Georgetown University Thursday wellness walk, led by Charles DeSantis.

Experience: When the First Exposure Went Wrong

If the user's first experience with a benefit program goes well, then things become much easier moving forward. As we discussed in Chapter 2, that positive first experience boosts the employee's knowledge and skills, and also makes future use of the benefit *feel more normal*. For both reasons, the employee will be more likely, generally, to continue using the benefit program.

If things didn't go well however, the future is much less promising. In tests we've run at HelloWallet with our own (financial wellness) program, we found it to be far hard to win back employees who tried our service and failed to continue using it, than it was to interest them in trying it out the first time.[119]

Solution 1: Break with Prior Experiences

If the first experience is negative, one option is to show employees that future experiences will be different — that what they experienced in the past simply isn't relevant because the program (or its delivery) is different.

For example, if a retirement planning session was panned by employees, enticing them to come back to another one will take more than sending out an email about the new event. And, assuring them "we've learned, it's better" likely won't be enough either. An employee's assessment is both deliberative ("System 2", considering costs and benefits) and nonconscious ("System 1", emotional, automatic, and based on associations). To get past the nonconscious *reaction*, the HR team must make the new program look and feel substantially different, so that the prior associations aren't activated. That may be completely different branding, a different person sending the communications, or a clearly different content or purpose for the seminar.

---

[119] See the whitepaper by Balz and Wendel (2014), which describes that test.

Solution 2: Move On

Sadly, the most viable, cost-effective option may simply be to move on — to stop trying to increase usage among the employees who had a bad experience. Instead, the team can devote scarce resources to and look for other targets of opportunity. Once employees are burned by a bad experience, it may be more difficult to restore their faith than to invest in future programs that avoid these problems altogether.

Solution 3: Avoid the problem

The best solution by far, of course, is to avoid the problem altogether. To make sure that employees don't have a negative first experience with the program — through thoughtful planning and, especially, through frequent testing and experimental optimization, as we've discussed the previous two chapters.

A Quick Recap

Many benefits suffer from low uptake and usage, even when the program is good for employees, and they want to use it. This chapter provides nuts and bolts techniques you can use to overcome these problems. Here's a summary of those techniques:

- ❖ Cues. If employees aren't using a program because of inattention (not being aware of it, forgetting, etc.), try to:
  - ○ Move into front of the employee's eye
  - ○ Highlight the single next step that's needed
  - ○ Try again (simple reminders)
- ❖ Reaction. If employees have a negative emotional or intuitive reaction, especially because they associate a new program with something uninteresting or unsuccessful in the past, try:
  - ○ Social Proof (Show that it's normal).
  - ○ Personalization
  - ○ Beautiful design

❖ Evaluation. If employees aren't clear about the costs and benefits for them, try to:

   o Highlight the most relevant benefits.

   o Make it a competition

   o Show them what they'll lose: Loss aversion

❖ Ability. If employees lack the resources or confidence to take action, or are blocked along the way, try to:

   o Make it easier

   o Decrease the number of options

   o Elicit Implementation Intentions

❖ Timing. If employees lack the urgency to take action now, try:

   o Accept Temporal Myopia & Focus on the Present

   o Use Incentives & Scarcity

   o Use Focal Dates and Deadlines

❖ Experience. If employees had a bad experience with the program before, try to:

   o Break with Prior Experiences

   o Move On

   o Avoid the problem

10
SPECIAL FOCUS: DELIVERING EFFECTIVE EMAIL COMMUNICATIONS

For many people, the location of a gym is a big factor in whether or not they actually sign up and go. Helping people find a gym near them can be immensely effective at increasing participation. Moreover, simply telling people they can *search* for a gym near them gets them more interested.

In an experiment run by Michel Aargaard, a simple change in email language from "get your membership" to "find your gym & get membership" *tripled* the number of people who clicked on the email to find out more.[120]

As you'll see in this chapter, it's not unusual to find small changes that increase action by 200% in emails. Which is excellent news because email is by far the most important channel for most benefits communications.

---

[120] 200% *increase* = 300% the original impact = 3x. See Aargaard (2013)

Email Is the Most Important Channel

Email is the backbone of most benefits communication — it's cost-effective, increasingly ubiquitous in the lives of employees, personalizable, and two-way. It's also a channel where there has been tremendous practical research on how to support action. So, we'll focus on that for this chapter, and talk about other channels in the next chapter.

In the spirit of this book, this chapter on email is about complementing your existing skills: It'll focus on the behavioral aspects and experimental research that are available in the field. Along the way, I'll mention existing resources about on email layout, metrics and tracking packages, and HR-specific content areas like compensation communication.

We all know that internal communications have legal and pragmatic constraints that limit the freedom of the HR team to develop compelling messages. These constraints can be so overwhelming that we want to throw up our hands and say "that's the best we can do for now". In this chapter, we'll focus on how to do it right, from a data-driven behavioral perspective: how to develop communications that you're proud of, and that drive action — and how then work within some of the constraints that internal communications face.

Setting the Stage

In Chapter 3, we talked about ways to clarify the behavioral outcome for a benefit program — finding the final outcome that the company is looking for, and defining success and failure for the program. Here, we need to do the same for each particular email.

1. **Clarify the goals upfront.** What is the purpose of the particular benefits communication? How does it fit into the larger communications strategy, and, most importantly, what observable behavior is it intended to support?

2. **Define success and failure.** Given that behavioral goal, what would success entail? What would mean failure?

146

Check back in Chapter 3 for tips on how to specify each of these, as appropriate. From here on out, I'll assume you've already defined the goal of the communication and success and failure.

What Works in Email

Simply put, for a benefits email to have an effect, employees have to notice it, open it, click on its links, and act on it. While there are many facets that are unique to an HR context, that sequence of required actions is shared across many disciplines. And, it has been studied, ad nauseam, by tens of thousands of focused, well-trained and well-funded, data-driven people for over a decade: email marketers. While HR emails shouldn't "look" like email marketing campaigns, there's a great deal we can learn about *behavior* from the field experiments they've conducted. In fact, often their work is informed by the same experimental methods and behavioral science that we've already discussed in this book; though often for very different purposes than we have here.

Detailed Tactical Lessons

Email marketers have studied each facet of an email in great detail. As I noted in the beginning of this chapter, it's not usual to find huge swings in individual behavior due to changes in an email. For example, seemingly small changes in subject lines, headers and content can double the number of readers taking action based on a single email communication in experimental studies. Let's look at some of the core results from the marketing practitioner literature, which also appear to hold for benefits communications based on HelloWallet's own experimental testing.

Subject Line

❖ **Keep it short.** The rule of thumb in email marketing is that readers only look at the first 30-50 characters of an email subject line.[121] *Most* of what's written after that is skipped. There are two reasons for that. First, because people receive so many emails, and have so much else to do in their lives, that they have no choice but to skim. Second, because readers are increasingly using mobile devices to read email, where only the first 30 characters or so are visible.[122] So, keep the main point of the message in the first few words.[123]

❖ **Be specific.** Vague subject lines imply vague and uninteresting content. Sometimes mysterious subject lines pique people's interest, but they can also flop. In general, tell people clearly what the email is about.

❖ **Be personal.** Include the person's name, or something like their job title that shows it is actually relevant for them. There's no need (and it's a bad idea) to include truly personal information about them; but using someone's name is a nice balance — personal without being "creepy".

Sender Name

❖ **Use a real person's name.** Would you rather open an email from "Audrey" or "Benefits"? Most people open emails from people over impersonal entities. While email is too often used as a tool to blast out content, it's best used in a conversation. And the conversation starts with real people talking to each other. Whenever possible, use the name of a person that employees actually know and like!

❖ **Make sure it's official and trustworthy.** Using a real person's name doesn't mean the email can't include the official branding of the company — it should. In most email clients, you can specify additional information like "Audrey, Retirement

---

[121] See https://whichtestwon.com/article-subject-line-test-results

[122] See http://masstransmit.com/broadcast_blog/mobile-email-from-name-and-subject-line-displays-infographic/

[123] Will add citation for an example AB test for each point; pending permissions.

Director." Also, readers will see that the email is coming from the official company domain.

Content Layout

❖ **Summarize the important stuff up front.** Depending on where employees are reading the email, they will initially see only the first XX-YY lines of the email in their window. Anything after that requires scrolling down — which takes work that's only worth the effort if the initial content is promising.

❖ **Keep paragraphs short, with subheadings for scanning.** People will often skim, and they skim from the left in an "F shaped" pattern (they read more of the first few lines, then often only the beginning word of later lines until they find something particularly interesting. Subheadings make it easy for people to jump to the part they are most interested in.[124]

❖ **Use interesting images and white space.** In particular, images of people catch the eye,[125] and break up blocks of text. Ample white space, around the header and images, also helps make it easier to read quickly.

Call to Action

Since communications are about action, and not just about transferring information, practitioners have focused special attention on the "Call to Action" (CTA), or the part(s) of the message that ask the reader to click or otherwise do something.

❖ **Place a clear CTA above the fold.** For many readers, the initial summary or even subject line is enough — they are cued and ready to go. So, make it easy for them to find out what to do next — put the link or button for the next step above "the

---

[124] Ideally, they would read each benefits email, from start to finish. Since that doesn't happen in practice (and there's no point trying to "make" people do it), we need to adapt to how they actually do read.

[125] See https://whichtestwon.com/medalias-painter-profile-picture-test

fold": the part they can see without scrolling, analogous to the top half of a folded newspaper.

❖ **Encapsulate the CTA.** Make the CTA clear and easy to find by separating it visually from the rest of the content — with white space or a box in a contrasting color.

❖ **Make it about the benefits of action.** The CTA is a tool to tell the reader *why* they should click. So, instead of saying "get started" or "continue", use CTAs like "Get my retirement match" or "Secure my health insurance." It's OK for the CTA to be a short phrase.

Time of Day and Day of Week

❖ **Tuesday and Thursday morning are most popular.** In general, the most frequently used times for emails are these two mornings; they are also the most frequent times for people to open emails. So, your email may get lost, but people do devote more time to email overall then. However, Saturdays and Sunday are much lower volume and, *in some tests*, show higher open and click rates, if your company is OK with sending email then.

❖ **Align with company policy and access times.** As the HR department, you know something that email marketers don't (though they wish they did) — which is when employees are at computers or otherwise accessible via email. Send then, or slightly before.

❖ **Timing matters: Plan on a short life-span.** The vast majority of email opens and clicks occur in the first hour after they are sent. So, the timing of the email really matters. While mid-week mornings generally best, timing is so important that you need to test what works best for your particular employees.

Size

❖ **Design for mobile.** More than 50% of emails opens now occur on mobile devices,[126] and new benefits emails must "work" on mobile. That *doesn't* mean you should include a link to a mobile version of the email — it means ensuring that the email is automatically easy to read on mobile. There are two ways to do this:[127] Making the email scalable, so the text and buttons are readable on mobile, or making them "responsive". Responsive emails automatically adjust to the size of the device they are on — and are the best option if your team can invest in the tools or skills to develop them. Note, mobile devices *may* not be an issue at present if you are using corporate email and restricting access to corporate email outside of the office.[128]

❖ **Don't go larger than 600 pixels wide.** Even for desktop email, the maximum default width for email viewing is 600 pixels; if you use a template that is wider than that, you're requiring that people scroll horizontally to read your message. That's frustrating, and you'll lose many of your readers.

❖ **Remember download times.** Since many people are accessing their email mobile devices, be mindful of how long it takes to download the email itself — and avoid using high resolution graphics or videos.

Strategic Lessons about Email Content

In terms of the content of the message itself, and what the subject line actually says, here are some of the broader, more strategic lessons from the marketing and behavioral science literatures. We can organize them according to the CREATE Action Framework:

---

[126] See https://litmus.com/blog/mobile-opens-hit-51-percent-android-claims-number-3-spot

[127] See Marketo, How to Design your Emails. http://www.marketo.com/_assets/uploads/How-to-design-your-emails.pdf

[128] However, that restriction itself is a major obstacle, as we'll discuss later.

Cue

❖ **The email itself serves as the initial cue for action.** But, as with any cue, it competes for attention with others. So, that's why the subject line (and sender name) is so important; see above. Within the email, the CTA is the cue for the next action (clicking, accessing the benefits website, etc.) — that's why making it easily accessible is key. It's also why you don't want to clutter an email with multiple competing CTAs.

❖ **Ask for action; don't imply it.** Especially with the CTA, it's OK to say directly what is needed next: "Click here to get your benefit" instead of "continue".

Reaction

❖ **Know your employees, and avoid baggage-laden phrases.** Readers can't help but have an immediate, intuitive reaction to the information you're presenting — even if there is a clear value proposition. So, steer clear of known triggers.

❖ **The email has to look professional.** In most cases, that means a simple text email, or a well-designed but not overwhelming HTML email. Professionalism is deeply linked to trust. But, professional does not necessarily mean a heavily designed marketing brochure — just something that people will intuitively trust as authentic and well-crafted.

❖ **Avoid stilted language and legal jargon.** Readers will associate it with boring, irrelevant content *even if it is not.* A great way to make the language conversational and sensible to your readers is to simply ask one of the targeted employees how they would describe it themselves, and put it in their words.

❖ **Personalize the look and feel.** We have an intuitive assessment of whether something is relevant to us or not — which includes whether the people displayed in an email look like us or our situation. The stereotypical example is for retirement planning: Showing images of young people just out of college (and just starting to save for retirement) isn't going to appeal to older people who are preparing to start retirement.

Evaluation

❖ **Make the benefit to them clear.** Why should the reader take action? What's the value it provides to them? As we discussed in Chapter 2, make sure that value is something immediate or near-term, and not something far in the future.

❖ **Personalize the value proposition.** You know a lot about your employees and their needs and interests. Instead of blasting the same email to everyone, tailor the message for particular people and groups who have *told you* what they want. We'll talk more about segmentation below.

Ability

❖ **Make sure they have what they need to act.** If you're asking someone to log into their benefits portal, are they likely to have the user name and password they need? If not, provide a link to retrieve it.

❖ **Tell them it's quick (if it is).** If the action is only going to take a few minutes, make sure to say so. Those simple lines you see in many marketing emails about "it'll only take three minutes" actually work.

Timing

❖ **Make urgent if possible.** Deadlines — like open enrollment — are one way to make a message urgent. If there is an existing deadline, nicely remind people of it. Time-restricted incentives, like a free iPad for the first 10 people who sign up, also create a sense of urgency — though this approach has other problems we'll revisit.

❖ **Make it immediate.** Readers care more about events occurring now, than those occurring in the future. For example, in an experiment which tested the effect of an email announcing a new event that was "Live Today:" versus "Live Tomorrow:", the today version had three times the event registrations. [129]

❖ **Make it timely.** When deciding to send out a message, one quick test is to ask: When would I most want to read and act on this? If it's an email about a new wellness program, would I want to receive it in the middle of winter holidays while I'm spending time with family (probably not), or right afterwards — around New Year's when I'm trying to set resolutions and figure out how to keep them?

Experience

❖ **Don't send the same content twice.** Every time you ask for action (i.e., send a benefits communication), people learn and subtly change because of your appeal for action. If you sending a communication that's identical to a previous one (especially if they already took action the first time) — you're teaching them that the first communication wasn't important. The new version doesn't have to be radically different, but it should work in the context of the *conversation over time* you're having with employees across communication. It would be strange to walk up to someone and say the exact same thing twice; as it is with email.

❖ **Remember: You're not communicating with the same person.** Even outside of benefits communications, every day, people are changing and adapting — in universal ways (aging) and idiosyncratic ways (getting married, having children, etc.). The person you emailed six months ago about their retirement plan is different from the person you're communicating with now. As a member of the HR team, you have unique insight into what might have changed

---

[129] See https://whichtestwon.com/brighttalks-timing-test-results

in the person's life. If the company has had a retirement workshop in the time since the last retirement communication, build on that. Especially if you can segment the communication to target those who attended.

Use the techniques from Chapter 8. In that chapter, we talked about general ways to get attention, create a sense of urgency, etc. While you're deploying email-specific lessons like "design for mobile", don't forget that the content itself can use tools like social proof, peer comparisons and incentives, too!

Evaluate Before It Goes Out

As a quick way to review your email, or to decide between alternative versions of an email you're considering, you can use the CREATE Action Funnel as a checklist, like this:

Does the email...	Email 1	Email 2
Cue to think about taking action	✔	✔
Create a positive Emotional Reaction	✔	✔
Support the Conscious Evaluation of costs and benefits	✔	✔
Ensure the Ability to act (resources, logistics, self-efficacy)	✘	✔
Provide Timing and urgency to act	✘	✘

Segmentation and Targeting

A core lesson from the behavioral sciences is that people are diverse, and face different obstacles to action. While we all have a similar decision-making process (the CREATE Action funnel), where, exactly, we get stuck depends on who we are and our histories. Email marketers have similarly discovered that emails meant to engender action are more effective when they are targeted to the particular experiences and needs of their audiences. The old days of blasting out the same email to everyone are largely gone: modern email campaigns are tailored to two or more subgroups within a population.

As HR professionals, you have unique knowledge that can make your content more tailored and meaningful for your employees. As Jennifer Benz, head of Benz Communications puts it nicely:

> *"Marketers would kill for the information you have at your fingertips... And, you can use this information to help people make good decisions and help your programs be successful."*[130]

Naturally, some of the knowledge you may have about individuals is off limits, for solid ethical and legal reasons. Beyond that, you can and should use your knowledge to have an intelligent and informed conversation with employees via your email. Think about it this way: if you walked up to an employee who you *knew* was already contributing the maximum that they could to a dependent FSA, why would you ever ask them to contribute more? You'd look like a fool, and you'd be wasting their time. But, we do that all the time with email — by sending out emails that we *know* are irrelevant to some recipients or ignore what they've already told us.

You can categorize employee knowledge into three areas:

- ❖ **Demographic information.** Age, income, location, etc.

- ❖ **Benefits status.** What benefits have people already signed up for? Are they contributing up to their limit for retirement or FSAs?

---

[130] See Benz (2014)

❖ **Behavioral history.** What email have they opened in the past? What workshops have they attended?

For an initial (one-size-fits-all) email, think briefly about who is likely to respond differently to the email. For whom would the one-size-fits-all email be insulting or completely irrelevant? Maybe it's something obvious: like newly hired young employees who really aren't going to be interested in a seminar about post-retirement annuities. Or maybe it's something you've learned in your day-to-day work that encapsulates your unique experience and insight. Perhaps new employees rarely show up to company social events because they don't feel comfortable yet — and need additional encouragement. Benz Communications has a nice summary of the different *ways* in which you can customize your messages,[131] from targeted messaging (one message for each segment of the population) all the way to variable messaging and calculations based on the particular employee's demographic and personal characteristics.

The segmented emails can, and often should, provide the same core information. In an HR context, it's often unfair and illegal not to tell every employee about a new benefit or benefit-related event. But, depending on the context, you don't necessarily have to deliver that information in the exact same way — the exact same subject line, same design, etc. You can highlight the announcement (and related action) that a particular group of employees is most likely to be interested in.

Once you've identified different groups of people who are likely to respond very differently, and who likely need a different approach, *test* those assumptions. Ask some of the employees what they think about a new design or different way to communicate the ideas. Develop the new design in full, and decide on how exactly it should be targeted (what data in the HR system should be used to generate a list for each email).

---

[131] See Benz (2014), a series of webinars on benefits communications tactics.

Here are a few quick tips:

- ❖ **Very few emails should be sent exactly the same way to all employees**, unless there are absolute legal requirements to do so. Remember, legally required *content* like disclosures doesn't necessarily mean the exact same presentation — legally required content can and must be included in the email template. But, the presentation and order of information can be tailored to the real needs and interests of your employees.

- ❖ **Don't ask people to do things they've already done**. Instead move them up the ladder of engagement. The most basic form of targeting is to filter out people who have already acted on prior emails or notices. If someone has already signed up for a wellness program, don't ask them to sign up; you can either not re-email those people (OK) or you can congratulate them and suggest a follow-up action (better).

- ❖ **You'll be surprised about who is interested in what.** As noted above, you should test your assumptions as you're developing the emails — by asking different groups of employees what they think about an email before you send it. But, even then, you should expect to be surprised. You'll find people who really like a program (and an email around it) that seemed non-obvious. Some of this feedback and learning can come from direct contact with employees; some of it needs to come from a good email tracking package.

Experimentation

Good email systems also make it very, very easy to experimentally test which version of an email works better than another one. As behavioral researchers and email marketers and have often found — small changes can have massive (2x, 3x) impacts on how readers respond to the message and whether they take action. And because of the inherent complexities of people, and the differences from one person to another, you simply can't know ahead of time which version will always be better.

Remember in Chapter 7, where we talked about the importance of ensuring that your vendors run experimental tests, and how pre/post analyses or other less-sophisticated but common techniques can provide misleading results? You can run experimental tests yourself — often with a simple click of a button in a modern mass email system. Packages like MailChimp, Cheetah Mail, HubSpot, and Marketo allow you to run "A/B" tests (experiments) on your emails — sending out two versions of the email at the same time to a randomly selected treatment and control group. You can then quickly tell which version of the email was most effective — and settle debates in the office. As an added bonus, these packages also tell you lots of useful information like whether employees were opening the email on web or mobile clients, the time of day, how many times they opened it or clicked on it, and (sometimes) even if they forwarded it on to other employees.

If your mail system doesn't automatically support experiments, you have two options. First, you ask your company to upgrade the system to one that does (that's the best option!) It's software that can help you increase the usage of most benefit program by up to 2x — that should generate a compelling ROI argument in favor. Second, you can actually run them yourself, with a bit of help. You, or someone on your team, would need to create two randomly assigned groups of employees, and then send the two versions of the email you want to test to them. It's beyond the scope of this book, but there are lots of tutorials online for running email A/B tests (including a section in my previous book, *Designing for Behavior Change*).

A Quick Recap

❖ Email is often the most important tool you have to engender action on employee benefits — it's cost-effective, increasingly ubiquitous among employees, employees have an existing habit of reading it, it's two-way, and it can provide detailed quantitative feedback so you can improve your effectiveness over time.

❖ Key tactical lessons from the experts in email effectiveness (email marketers) include: Use short subject lines, a personal and trustworthy sender name, key content in the first *short* paragraph, an encapsulated call to action that tells users what they'll receive, and weekday morning emails, especially Tuesdays and Thursdays.

❖ Strategic lessons about the content of email can be organized around the CREATE Action funnel — create professional looking emails that don't trigger an intuitive negative reaction, personalize them with pictures and recipient names, make sure they have the ability to act on the email immediately, and make the content timely and, if possible, urgent.

❖ Don't bore or insult your readers — use the knowledge you have about them to create segmented, targeted emails for their interests and needs

❖ Good email packages support experimental testing — to really understand what changes in your email are effective. If you don't already have one that does, ask for it!

11

OBSERVING THE ROLLOUT AND NAVIGATING THE CHALLENGES

In Chapter 6, we discussed how you can evaluate evidence that vendors provide about their programs, before you buy them. After you've rolled out a benefits intervention you can go through a very similar process to determine whether it has worked! Rather than repeating all of the commentary and caveats covered in Chapter 6, this section will provide a quick summary and point out unique issues.

In order to make solid judgments about whether a benefits intervention worked out as planned or not, and to figure out what to do next, there are two distinct considerations:

1. Instrumentation: Are you tracking the data you need?

2. Evaluation: Can you tell what was *caused* by the intervention?

Of course, things will rarely work out exactly as planned. If the impact of the intervention is less than hoped, then two additional questions arise:

1. What obstacles seem to have decreased the intervention's impact?

2. What can we do about it?

The first type questions — data tracking and causality — form the Observe stage of the ACTION model; the latter two — obstacles and responses — form the final, Navigate stage.

Instrumentation: Are you tracking the data you need?

Measure Outcomes First

It seems simplistic, but it's something we all stumble over: Make sure you're measuring the outcomes you really care about. If you care about your employee's financial preparation for medical emergencies, ensure that the program actually measures that, and not something else that might be related to it. For example, measure their actual *contributions* to their HSAs, and not how financially prepared they *feel*. In most cases, participation, engagement, and satisfaction — all common metrics that HR departments examine — aren't the final outcomes that they really care about. They are useful precursors, but potentially misleading without a metric of the actual final outcome.

Where possible, invest upfront in tools and procedures that make gathering data and evaluating programs quick and easy. In Chapter 2, we discussed how small frictions — like an extra form to fill out — can stop employees from taking action on their benefits. The same lesson applies to *us* too, in the benefits space. If we find it difficult or time consuming to gather data about our programs' impact, we won't do as thorough of a job and won't gain as much insight into our employees. Where possible, look for tools in which the data gathering is fully automated, and immediately available. Automated exercise trackers like the FitBit provide a good example of that.

Measure Each Small Step Leading Up To It

Despite your best efforts, your interventions will work for some employees, and not others. Some employees won't take action — whether it's contributing to a retirement account, picking a health plan that's best suited to their family's needs, or enrolling in career advancement program.

In order to understand *why* an intervention didn't work for some employees, we need to know *where* they got stopped. Did employees simply not read the email? Did they get to the benefits portal and couldn't figure out what to do next? Did they simply decide the program wasn't right for them? We want to separate out those who wanted to take action but failed to, from those who sincerely weren't interested.

That process starts by instrumenting each small step the employee would take between first learning about the intervention and actually taking action. That might be opening an email or seeing a poster, going to a website, meeting with the HR team, etc. We want to gather data about each interaction the employee has with the program. That's true whether you're just sending out an email about an existing benefit, or rolling out a completely new program with a large-scale awareness raising campaign. We want to create what's known in the marketing literature as a *conversion funnel.*

Let's say you're rolling out a new health insurance exchange (public or private). A conversion funnel for this rollout would trace each major step along the way from initially telling employees about the exchange to their actual signing up for plans. The funnel tells you where along the process you're losing people — are you not getting their attention with the initial message? Are they not going to the exchange site? Or are they going to the site, but failing to sign up for a plan?

The funnel for this new health insurance exchange is shown in Figure 14.

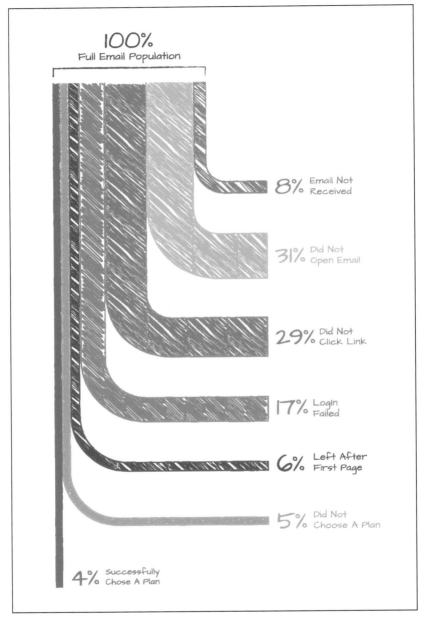

Figure 14: An easy way to visualize where employees are dropping off, with a conversion funnel

This start-to-finish picture is essential for improving the effectiveness of a benefit package.

An Example: Instrumenting Email

As discussed in the previous chapter, email is the single most powerful interaction that many HR teams have with their employees, and the key factor in whether employees actually use their benefits or not. So, let's dig into the particular data you'd want to collect when sending out an email about a new benefit program, accessible via a benefits portal. To keep things short, we'll just look at the email side; you'll want to instrument the benefits portal also, as was shown in Figure 14.

Aggregate Click Rates

For many benefits emails, there will be a digital action that you're asking people to take — like logging into their benefits portal. The simplest feedback you can get on these emails is their click rate — what proportion of your readers actually opened the email and decided to take the action suggested in the email. Modern email systems can report those rates. You can then compare click rates across emails, and, especially, across multiple versions of the same email, to see what works for your employees and what doesn't.

Aggregate Open Rates

Similarly, many email systems will also report open rates — the percent of people that appeared to open an email. Relative to click rates, however, open rates are generally less reliable and less useful; though they can still provide valuable information. They can help you determine if people simply aren't opening the email, and the subject lines, sender names and email timing catch people's attention. Opening an email is a necessary first step to clicking on it.

However, there are two things to watch out for when working with open rates. First, they are often measured with a special, tiny image placed in the email — when the recipient opens the email, it loads the image and the sender's email system records that fact. But, if recipients *block* images, like some email clients do by default, the tracking system doesn't work — and you then really don't know whether people opened the email or not. Thankfully, some corporate email systems can track email opens via other means, and escape that particular problem; your company's IT team would know whether effective email open tracking is available.

The second challenge with open rates is that they are a "shallow metric" — they can be misleading on their own. As we've discussed above, you generally want people to take action based on the email, not simply read it. So, you don't want to get too excited about open rates, if the click rates don't match up.

Click to Open Rates

Click to open rates tell you what portion of people who opened the email actually clicked on its link to take action. This is a very useful statistic because it tells you how well the content of the email delivered on the promise represented by the subject line. Did the subject line entice people but the content bored them? You'll see low click to open rates.

Individual Level Data

Ideally, your email system should be able to provide you with more than aggregate statistics — it should be able to show who, precisely, clicked on or opened an email. That's not so you can look at information about individuals directly (that's not useful in general and it violates employee privacy), but so you can do better segmentation and email design in the future.

Here's how it works:

❖ If your email system can track individual level information, that information would be linked to employee IDs or email addresses.

❖ Add open/click data to your larger data set about employees, including what benefits they are enrolled in and what their personal characteristics are.

❖ Compare the email behavior of diverse groups within your population. This can occur with simple averages by age, job title, or prior benefits enrollment, or with a more advanced statistical model.

❖ Determine which data best separate those who responded well to the email versus those who didn't, and label those segments in your data set.

❖ Develop new emails that better address the needs of underserved employees.

❖ Send out the new emails, and keep refining your understanding of which types of employees like which types of information and email presentation.

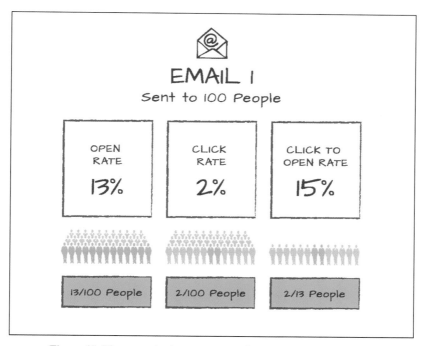

Figure 15: How to calculate your most important email statistics

Evaluation: Can you tell what was *caused* by the intervention?

It's important to track the outcomes you care about — but unfortunately that isn't enough. How do you know that your intervention — like a debt management program — actually helped employees? Maybe the people who signed up for the debt management program are just the people who had the personal commitment and wherewithal to pay off their debts on their own?

In Chapter 6, Evaluating Vendor Programs, we covered the core challenges to figuring out whether a vendor's program actually works before you buy it:

1. **Problems with *asking* employees about impact.** Employees who answer surveys often don't represent those who do not. People subtly "stretch the truth", intentionally or unintentionally when they answer. And, unfortunately, people simply may not know what impact your intervention had on them versus everything else in their lives.

2. **Problems with how you infer impact.** Since surveys about impact are riddled with problems, you can measure behavior and outcomes directly instead. But, a common technique in the field — looking at employee outcomes before and after an intervention, or "pre/post" analyses — is deeply flawed, because it doesn't control for everything else in the employee's lives. Similarly, comparing enrolled versus non-enrolled employees is very misleading. And, sometimes, with external programs, vendors are tempted to cherry pick the data and make it seem like there is an impact when there isn't.

3. **Problem with measuring the wrong thing.** It's easy to measure participation, but it's a poor substitute for what most companies rarely really care about — impact on employee's lives. Measuring engagement is also challenging, because the term is used in vague ways (see Chapter 12).

The same lessons also apply, unfortunately, after the fact. They apply for any type of benefits intervention — whether it's an email the HR team sends to employees, a benefits fair, a new internally managed benefit, or a vendor-supplied one. There are simply lots of way to trip up, thinking that a program is having an impact when it really isn't.

There are approaches that HR teams can take — and require from their vendors or internal IT teams. The most rigorous and conceptually simple of these is the **staggered rollout:** Some randomly selected employees get the benefit program or email on Day One, and the rest receive it at some later date. By comparing those two randomly selected groups, employers can know for sure that nothing, other than the benefits intervention itself, led to differences in outcomes between the two groups.

In the health space especially, sophisticated vendors and researchers use an additional technique — propensity score matching — to approximate a randomized experiment and the clarity it provides. When it works, it gives a solid measure of a program's impact. It requires careful data gathering and tracking though, and there are more opportunities to trip up and get misleading results.

Navigating the Challenges that Arise

Assuming things don't go perfectly with the intervention, then the question naturally arises — well, what next? To be clear, the goal of the ACTION spiral is avoid this question as much as possible. We've sought to *fail fast*: pulling failures from the future into the present, and fixing them before they are expensive and embarrassing. But some do inevitably occur.

What obstacles seem to have decreased the intervention's impact?

In the Observe step, we made sure we were measuring each small step the employee could take, stating with their first interaction with the benefits intervention on (usually: receiving an email from HR).

We can then look at the *conversion funnel*, as shown in Figure 14, to see where employees are getting stopped.

To understand *why* they are getting stopped, we turn back to the CREATE funnel, discussed in Chapter 2. The CREATE funnel describes six main obstacles that can occur — from a lack of attention to a lack of urgency to a negative first experience. With this framework in mind, talk with employees who didn't take action and try to understand why they struggled, or test assumptions about why they struggled as described in Chapter 7.

What can we do about it?

Chapters 9 (tactics for uptake and usage) and 10 (email tactics) provide detailed lessons about how to help employees overcome behavioral obstacles, mapped to the CREATE funnel. With an understanding of which obstacle employees are facing, the HR team can then try the techniques outlined in those two chapters, brainstorm additional ideas, and discover in practice how to better serve the needs of employees and the company.

Implicit in this approach is an understanding that no benefit program is ever perfect in the first try. Neither is any email, poster, or employee benefit competition. That is why the ACTION model is a spiral — the possibility of further iteration and improvement is always there. It's up to the HR team to decide when a particular program succeeds well enough to move on to more pressing topics.

A Quick Recap

❖ Observing the outcome of a benefits intervention consists of two stages, setting up systems to gather data (instrumenting), and evaluating the results.

❖ Talk with your IT team (or vendor) to gather data about the final outcomes — employee wellness, retirement contributions etc. — as well as each small step along the way. For example, for an email announcing a new benefit, gather data about whether employees open the email, click on it, log into the benefits portal, sign up, etc. That start to finish data is known as a *conversion funnel*.

❖ Recall from Chapter 6 that not all data about the impact of a benefit program can be trusted; it's just too easy to be misled by bad data that's measured incorrectly or interpreted loosely. Staggered rollouts (via random selection) offer one rigorous and straightforward way to ensure the HR team gets a clear understanding.

❖ Throughout this book, we've tried to find problems early, before they occur during the full rollout of a benefits intervention. But, some issues will inevitably occur — and we can navigate them as they arise.

❖ The *conversion funnel*, combined with the CREATE model from Chapter 2 can help the HR team figure out where and why (respectively) employees fail to take action.

❖ No program is perfect, and it may take a few iterations until a program succeeds. That is what the ACTION model is a spiral — each iteration we can learn and improve our programs, to make them better serve employees and the company.

12

SPECIAL FOCUS: UNDERSTANDING EMPLOYEE ENGAGEMENT

"Employee engagement" is a term often thrown around as a key outcome of employee benefits. Everything from wellness programs[132] to pet insurance[133] to brain-training games[134] are said to increase engagement. If your team decided that employee engagement is a key outcome of your program during the assessment process covered in the last two chapters, then it's important to dig in and make sure everyone is on the same page on what employee engagement means. This chapter reviews the research on employee engagement and how it can be (and isn't) affected by their benefits.

What is Employee Engagement?

First, let's get clear on exactly what the company really wants. The term employee engagement became popular over the last 15 years in

---

[132] http://www.virginpulse.com/

[133] http://partners.healthypawspetinsurance.com/AffiliateAssets/RWOI

[134] http://www.workforce.com/articles/brain-training-is-becoming-the-new-push-in-employee-wellness

consulting and HR circles, and there seem to be three main ways the term is used:[135]

1. **Participation**. Sometimes "engagement" means simply *participating* in an employer program, such as attending a seminar, or signing up for a wellness program. This is a low bar that doesn't necessarily imply that the program is impactful or that employees value it.

2. **Emotional attachment to work**. "Engagement" can also mean an emotional commitment on the part of a person toward their job, which then translates into higher productivity, better customer service, and lower absenteeism. This is a definition used in business management and some academic studies.

3. **Something good**. "Engagement" is also used as a catch-all term for everything good and beneficial for a company that isn't quite tangible. For example, I've seen both productivity and employee satisfaction equated to engagement. In fact, a common complaint about the term "engagement" is that it mixes causes (good managers) with attitudes (feelings about the company), behaviors (discretionary effort) and outcomes (productivity).[136]

I prefer #2, **emotional attachment to work**; that's one of the most widely used formal definitions, and the one that I find to be the most clear and concise. It's the emotional state that is *caused* by a

---

[135] There are numerous related concepts in the academic community, such as organizational citizenship, which I touch upon below. Since the term "employee engagement" arose in the HR consulting community, here I am focusing on that term and how it is used; I'll reference the academic literature and concepts where relevant to the concept of engagement. Unfortunately, there isn't consensus within the academic community on what this or related terms mean either: E.g. Schaufeli and Bakker (2010), Weiss (2002)

[136] E.g., Macey and Schneider (2008).

supportive work environment, and *causes* behaviors and outcomes such as increased productivity.[137]

The emotional attachment to one's work, or employee engagement as we have defined it, shouldn't be confused with other employee characteristics like:

❖ **Motivation.** When HR professionals refer to motivation, they usually mean an employee's extrinsic reason to do something — the desire to get paid, to be recognized, and to complete a task. And, because of that focus, there's a lot of talk in the HR community about providing *incentives* to make employees "more motivated". Engagement is different — and adding incentives is largely ineffective (and often detrimental, as we'll talk about later). Instead of the fickle, coin-operated meaning that's often attached to motivation, engagement is an internal and relatively stable emotional bond.

❖ **Satisfaction.** Many Americans are *satisfied* with work, but not engaged. According to SHRM, 83% of American workers are satisfied, but only 30% of them are engaged, according to Gallup.[138] How can that be? While the two concepts are strongly related, these surveys are clearly measuring different things. Employee satisfaction can be considered a basic level of contentment with one's job; engagement is a more recent and richer concept that extends far beyond satisfaction.[139] As

---

[137] There's a similar distinction in the academic literature between core personality traits and environment factors that then cause persistent psychological attitudes (like I'm calling engagement, here) and states, which are more transient. They then cause job performance characteristics, like putting in extra time at work, etc.

[138] Gallup (2013a). This is especially striking because Gallup's survey was previously considered a survey of "job satisfaction" before it was rebranded. It's the measurement of "engagement" that effectively defines it; there is no formal definition. And clearly, these two surveys are measuring (and defining) two different things. In the academic community "job satisfaction" has a particular and narrower definition; I'm using the non-technical meaning of the term here.

[139] Engagement, as used here, is related to the concept of "*overall* job satisfaction" (E.g., Weiss 2002), as distinct from "job satisfaction" and

Abhishek Mittal from Towers Watson describes it, "Satisfaction is a 'one-way street' (what can you do for me), whereas engagement is a 'two-way street' (what can you do for me and what I can do in return)"[140] Perhaps most importantly, engagement is strongly correlated with increased productivity, while satisfaction is less so.

❖ **Happiness.** Happiness is a current emotional state that is often related to many factors that have nothing to do with employment — the weather (people are happier on sunny days), family life, personality, etc. Engagement is viewed as a more enduring emotional attachment. An employee can be happy because he just ate a great bagel; that bagel doesn't mean much for employee engagement.

To better understand employee engagement, and how it works, let's look at four questions:

❖ Why is it important?

❖ How is it measured?

❖ What causes it?

❖ How does one improve it?

Why Is It Important?

Now that we have an answer for what employee engagement really is, let's move on to what outcomes employers can realistically expect if engagement *does* increase. Over the years, employee engagement has been the subject of numerous research studies. According to a Gallup survey of 1.4 million employees, teams scoring in the top

---

"cognitive job satisfaction". Trying to keep that distinction clear is difficult with such similar terms, though. Using "engagement" is clearer.

[140] See Mittal (2011). The "one way-street" metaphor fits one of the most common theoretical frameworks to understand employee satisfaction — Locke's Affect Theory (1976).

25% of respondents for engagement have the following characteristics, relative to those in the bottom 25%[141]

❖ 65% lower turnover (in industries with low-turnover normally)

❖ 48% fewer safety incidents

❖ 41% fewer quality incidents (i.e., defects)

❖ 37% lower absenteeism

❖ 28% less "shrinkage" (i.e., theft at work)

❖ 21% higher productivity

❖ 22% higher profitability

❖ 10% higher customer metrics

Beyond workplace outcomes, Gallup also argues that engagement is positively related to employee physical health (lower diabetes, obesity, and blood pressure rates) and healthy habits as well (exercising regularly eating healthier). While these relationships come from surveys that *correlate* engagement with positive employee outcomes, and don't show that engagement directly causes them, the general sense in the field is that engagement plays a causal, though difficult to measure, role.

In terms of dollars and cents, a study by Kenexa of 39 employers found that companies ranking in the top quartile of employee engagement had seven times higher total shareholder returns over five years than those in the bottom quartile (19% versus -4%), and twice the annual net income.[142]

For employers, employee engagement writer Kevin Kruse highlights what may be the single-most important outcome from employee engagement, which drives many of the other outcomes described above: discretionary effort.

---

[141] Gallup (2013b). See Harter et al. (2002) for a meta-analytic review across business units for the Gallup data that comes to similar conclusions.

[142] See Kenexa (2009)

For example, he says:

> *"...the engaged retail clerk picks up the trash on the store floor, even when the boss isn't watching...the TSA agent will pull a suspicious bag to be searched, even if it's the last bag on their shift."[143]*

A simple way of thinking about the impact of engagement is this: Look at the negative. Someone who is disengaged (by definition) isn't attached to their work. How would you expect someone to act who didn't want to work at their job? They wouldn't work very hard. They would find creative excuses not to come in. They wouldn't be very pleasant with customers. They would take opportunities to stay home or do other things when presented (snow days = days off instead of working from home). Eventually, they would quit. And that's basically what researchers have argued.[144]

How is it measured?

Employee engagement is a mental state — it's something in our heads and hearts that represents the attachment we feel to our work.[145] It's something that can't be observed directly, and is at the intersection of various complex internal processes and emotions. Nevertheless, researchers have tried to draw out this complex internal state and put a name and number on it, because whatever "it" really is, it's clearly quite important.

---

[143] Kruse (2012), http://www.forbes.com/sites/kevinkruse/2012/06/22/employee-engagement-what-and-why/,

[144] For example, one line of research in the academic community defines engagement as the opposite of burnout. See Maslach et al. (2001).

[145] This follows the "state engagement" definition from Macey and Schneider (2008). Also, this definition effectively mixes the two type of engagement Saks (2006) employs of "job engagement" and "role engagement."

Researchers usually measure engagement with surveys. One of the most popular surveys, Gallup's Q12 survey,[146] asks participants about their personal feelings and characteristics of their workplace environment that are correlated with engagement.[147] For example, their questions include:

- ❖ "In the last year, I have had opportunities at work to learn and grow."

- ❖ "My supervisor, or someone at work, seems to care about me as a person."

- ❖ "I know what's expected of me at work."

- ❖ "My associates or fellow employees are committed to doing quality work." [148]

Other surveys attempt to focus just on the emotional attachment itself, and ask employees about it. The Utrecht Work Engagement Scale,[149] commonly used in academic research, asks:

- • "At my work, I feel bursting with energy."

- • "My job inspires me."

- • "I am proud of the work that I do."

- • "I am immersed in my work."

Since engagement is a term to summarize a complex internal state, there's no single standard metric for it. Gallup's Q12 survey appears

---

[146] Gallup (2014), in particular: https://q12.gallup.com/Public/en-us/Features?ref=hoxmepage.

[147] Thus, while the Gallup survey is popular, it's far from perfect because it mixes, and potentially confuses, various levels and definitions of "engagement".

[148] Keep in mind though that these research studies don't necessarily use the same definition of *engagement* — since engagement is both an internal intangible state and an at-times fuzzy concept that has arisen in the consulting community, there is no single "real" definition; practitioners and researchers define engagement by how they measure it, and they measure it differently.

[149] See Schaufeli (2014); Schaufeli et al. (2006)

to be the most widely used, but it's certainly not universal. With it and other surveys, however, there's no way to interpret the results *on their own*. An engagement score of "2" doesn't actually mean anything. It's only by comparing other companies or other time periods *with the same survey* can you tell relative engagement. That means: Be very careful when comparing engagement across companies if they aren't using the exact same survey under the exact same circumstances, or across programs that are supposed to improve engagement if they aren't using the same survey and circumstances. Differences in how the survey is defined and administered are likely to have a much greater impact on the numbers than a particular benefit program or company policy.

How can it be improved?

Researchers and practitioners have promoted various approaches to improving employee engagement. The strongest empirical work comes from related, and much older, research traditions such as job satisfaction, job involvement, and organizational commitment; however, some recent work has also been conducted on employee engagement specifically.[150]

It short, engagement is driven by a mix of objective factors (work conditions, pay, etc.), more intangible factors at work (treatment by supervisors and colleagues), and personal characteristics (personality, genetic predispositions, home situation, etc.). To improve it however, there are three places to focus your efforts:

1. The work environment where someone does their job.

2. The job the person is doing.

3. The person who's doing the job.

---

[150] Most of what we know comes from surveys of engagement (and satisfaction, etc.), and what engagement is correlated to, instead of things that it conclusively causes. That said, engagement is related of a variety of factors, both in the workplace and beyond, as described here.

Create a Supportive Workplace

Start with Direct Supervisors

To a large extent, whether one has an engaging work environment or not is determined by whom you directly report to and work with on a daily basis. Gallup's CEO Jim Clifton states that "the single biggest decision you make in your job...is who you name manager. When you name the wrong person manager, nothing fixes that bad decision. Not compensation, not benefits — nothing."[151] Les McKeown, author and CEO of Predictable Success, puts it more event more bluntly: "The problem is with your managers, not your employees. If your employees are disengaged, your managers are at fault."[152]

Characteristics of a Supportive Environment

What is it that supervisors do to build engagement? In their review of the data on engagement, the UK's Institute for Employment Studies found that the key driver of engagement is "the sense of feeling valued and involved" with one's work.[153] The sense of feeling valued comes from:

- ❖ Involvement in decision-making

- ❖ The ability to voice ideas, and be listened to

- ❖ Opportunities for growth

- ❖ The feeling that the organization is concerned for their employees well-being.

The employee's manager has a primary role in each of these areas, as does the leadership and HR team of the company. Author Paul Marciano posits that improving engagement means that company leaders need to promote a culture of RESPECT in the workplace,

---

[151] Gallup (2013a)

[152] McKeown (2012), http://www.inc.com/les-mckeown/stop-employee-engagement-and-address-the-real-problem-.html.

[153] Robinson et al. (2004)

where RESPECT is his acronym for the five key elements: "Recognition, Empowerment, Supportive Feedback, Partnering, Expectations, Consideration, and Trust."[154] While other researchers use different terms, these are common themes. For example, Gallup argues that to improve engagement, hire, promote, or train managers who genuinely care for their people, invest in talent, and creatively motivate employees towards clear metrics.[155]

Create Supportive Jobs

The Job Itself Must Be Meaningful and Interesting

Beyond creating an environment in which people feel valued, certain core characteristics of people's jobs drive engagement. First and foremost: employees must feel that the job itself is meaningful to the organization, and contributes to the goals of the organization.[156] Researchers have identified a host of other job characteristics that contribute to engagement.[157] The work itself should:

❖ Be interesting and challenging

❖ Have variety

❖ Allow the use of different skills

❖ Allow personal discretion (autonomy)

There is a vast body of research behind various job characteristics; in 1976, Locke noted that at least 3,600 studies had been conducted as of that point in time on the influence of job characteristics on employee performance and topics related to engagement.[158]

---

[154] Marciano (2010)

[155] Not surprisingly, perhaps, Gallup has developed a proprietary metric for assessing a job candidate's likelihood of engaging his subordinates, called the Engagement Creation Index.

[156] Corporate Leadership Council (2004)

[157] Saks (2006), Citing Kahn (1992)

[158] Locke (1976)

However, these characteristics are some of the most common results in the literature.

Because engagement is driven in part by the nature of the work itself, some roles appear to be inherently more engaging than others. Managers are generally more engaged than non-managers, for example. That may be because managers can clearly see their purpose within the organization and usually have more autonomy than other employees. There are also significant differences occur across industries. An astounding 28% of transportation workers and 26% of manufacturing workers are considered "actively disengaged" (spreading dissent) but only 9% of physicians.[159]

What Must Not Occur

Variety, discretion and opportunities for growth are irrelevant if an employee feels the job site is unsafe or is harassed at work and feels that the employer is indifferent to their situation. A lack of organizational or supervisor support in the face of harassment can destroy engagement, as can these negative factors:

- ❖ Perceived injustice in how one is treated by supervisors

- ❖ Job site accidents and injury

- ❖ Inability to perform one's job (lack of skills or resources)

Satisfaction and engagement can be increased by ensuring that job sites are safe and comfortable, and do not overly fatigue the body. Ensure that job sites are safe and comfortable to safeguard satisfaction and engagement. Again, if employees are in danger, or don't have what they need to do their job well, other efforts to improve engagement are merely window dressing.

Changing the Jobs People Fulfill

Engagement author Paul Marciano also notes that in a highly disengaged workforce, resolution may require changes in staffing. While changes in staffing may seem extreme, it's important to note

---

[159] Gallup (2013a)

that engagement is, in large part, determined by relatively fixed characteristics of the individual and the job. Some researchers argue that dissatisfaction can arise from the inherent mismatch between what the job offers the individual versus what they want, and others that people's personalities differ in terms of how satisfied they will be at work overall.[160] In either case, efforts to change engagement without fundamentally changing the individual or the role can only go so far. Thus, high engagement starts with the right people in the right jobs for them.

The Role of Benefits in Creating an Engaging Environment

A common perspective in the benefits space is that engagement can be bought with compensation and perks — from better pay to special programs that claim to boost engagement (e.g., Virgin Pulse, Keas). But, there's disagreement about that in the research community.

Gallup, for example, flatly states that "indulging employees is no substitute for engaging them."[161] Gallup dismisses the role of hours expectations, vacation time, or working remotely full-time on employee engagement. It identifies only two policies — flextime and the ability to work remotely part-time that are positively related to engagement. Research from the Corporate Leadership Council also notes how many programs, from maternity leave to fitness programs to prescription drug benefits have relatively little impact on engagement.[162]

If the level of compensation per se doesn't promote engagement, nor do many benefits, what role does benefits play? *To date, there have been few scientific studies of the real impact of benefits on engagement.* But, by reviewing initial research by the Corporate Leadership Council[163] and

---

[160] See Affect Theory and Dispositional Theory.

[161] Gallup (2013a); p27

[162] Corporate Leadership Council (2004)

[163] Corporate Leadership Council (2004)

applying the broader literature on engagement, we can infer promising guidelines:

1) **Focus on how the benefits are communicated.** Communication can matter more than the benefits themselves. Clearly informing employees about the benefit they have helps employees see that, yes, the company is concerned with their welfare appears to be the single most powerful lever that benefits professionals have on engagement.

2) **Listen and respond to employee needs.** Figure out the benefits that employees want, and provide them. It sounds simple, but it's actually directly counter to the approach taken by many engagement programs: There isn't a magic engagement program that HR teams can buy. Benefits per se don't engage employees; it's the act of listening and responding to employee needs that is important. Ask employees what programs they want, and demonstrate that HR is listening. Similarly, actively ask for feedback on existing programs. HR may not always be able to deliver, but the act of seeking and listening to employee input helps create the supportive environment.

3) **Promote equitable interaction among employees and build social bonds.** For example, a wellness program that involves team work in a non-coerced, authentic environment can build engagement; a wellness competition in which insiders or management seem to win or pick the winners undermines the sense of justice and fairness that supports into engagement.[164]

Or, looking at these positive attributes from the other direction:

4) **Don't let benefits problems be a distraction.** Employees should feel that they are cared for, and listened to. While adding benefits may not magically increase engagement, poorly executing them (with bad communication, lack of alignment with employee's stated needs), can hurt.

---

[164] Saks (2006)

For example, in 2011 Plan Sponsor Magazine described how Delta Air Lines managed its merger with Northwest Airlines.[165] The two companies had disparate benefit programs, and employees were uncertain about what their packages would look like moving forward. The result was a potential nightmare from an employee engagement perspective.

Yet, that didn't happen. The HR team ensured that employees on both sides of the merger had frequent and clear communications about the future. Tahvonen and his team also undertook a "road show" around the country, spreading the word about the benefit programs, meeting with employees, and answering their questions. In an uncertain time, the benefits team found ways to turn around the situation and support employee engagement — showing employees of the newly merged company that the benefits team was available, listening, and working for them.

Tips on Improving Engagement

To fundamentally improve employee engagement, many of the changes needed are structural and not undertaken in an afternoon. These are long term concerns that a company builds into its practices. Here's what's needed:

❖ **Make sure your managers, and the organization, actually support their employees.** For most people, the quality of the work environment hinges on the tone set by their immediate managers, in how they interact with the employee directly and the environment they support among coworkers. That means giving employees the resources they need, providing clear direction, and involving them in decision making.

❖ **Make sure employees are doing meaningful work at which they can succeed.** If people are in jobs that are uninteresting or unimportant to the organization, or they

---

[165] See's "2011 Plan Sponsor of the Year Finalist: Delta Airlines Inc." http://www.plansponsor.com/blank.aspx?id=6442477931.

don't feel they can be successful, on average they won't try as hard.

❖ **Sincerely ask for what employees want, and give it to them where possible.** Engagement is at root an emotional attachment to a company — with strong correlation to the feeling that the company cares about them. But there's no universal way to show that the company is truly interested in their welfare; instead, it requires honest caring, listening to employees, and showing them that they are being listened to. It needn't (and often shouldn't) be touchy-feely — but employees need to see that the company is responsive to their needs and requests.

❖ **Stamp out hostile environments.** Above and beyond creating a positive environment, companies need to be on the lookout for engagement killers — things that poison the work environment. Harassment is near the top of the list — if an employee is being harassed (verbally, sexually, physically) at work, and the company isn't stopping it, they can't (and shouldn't) feel a positive attachment to their job. Similarly, the sense that they or a group they self-identify with are being discriminated against can kill an employee's attachment to their work.

Often you can't change the overall workplace environment and roles that people are in. But, there are still smaller things you can do to improve employee engagement — and build up the right atmosphere over time. Here are some places to start:

❖ **Measure where you are.** It's difficult to know what's working if you don't know where you're starting from. Doubtless, you'll already have a sense of your overall employee engagement from everyday interactions. But, by creating a repeatable external metric of engagement, you can track progress and distinguish effective and ineffective efforts. Clear metrics also help focus the management team's attention. Gallup's (proprietary) survey tool is the most commonly used in the field, but you can also devise your own.

❖ **Set goals.** Given a metric of where you are, set clear goals and hold senior leaders accountable to them. Remember, though, these goals and metrics are probably completely meaningless to most employees — it is the actions that the company takes to actually support its employees that matter, not the company's *intention* to be supportive. The goals and metrics are for senior leaders, to keep their feet to the fire. Again, engagement isn't a *program,* it's something that arises based on the other actions companies take.

❖ **Communicate clearly with employees.** For example, tell them about their benefits in ways that normal people can understand and value. To be frank, many official corporate communications don't exactly speak to an emotional bond between the individual and their employer.

❖ **Ask employees about problems in their work environment, and fix them.** Are there problems of harassment, job site safety, or lack of vital resources to be effective? Are there bad managers or employees who are poisoning the environment? Asking employees is important; companies must also remedy the problems and show that they responding to employee concerns.

A Quick Recap

❖ **Employee engagement is often claimed as an outcome of benefit programs**, but it's definition is too often fuzzy. The clearest one in the literature is: *An employee's emotional attachment to work.*

❖ **Employee engagement has significant relationships to employee productivity, turnover, and quality of work.** For example, top quartile companies in terms of engagement have 37% lower absenteeism than the bottom quartile of companies.

❖ **Little solid research has been conducted on the relationship between benefits and employee engagement,** to date. Most of the data out there is not rigorous and meaningful. That said, there are lessons we can draw from the research.

❖ **Specific benefit programs don't seem to affect engagement per se;** however listening to employee needs and clearly addressing them with appropriate benefits likely does increase engagement.

❖ **The key determinants of engagement are:** Support provided by one's immediate supervisor, the meaningfulness and value of the work being down, and the employee's ability to do the work. While not central, benefits can play a role by encouraging equitable relationships between employees and building social bonds.

13
WRAP UP

Recent research in the behavioral sciences can help HR teams increase the impact of their employee benefits. We can better understand the obstacles that employees face to using their benefits, and use techniques from the research — from loss aversion and peer comparisons to simple reminders — to help employees overcome those obstacles. The result, I hope, is a world in which benefit programs are more closely aligned to the needs of employees and their employers.

In this book, I've tried to provide a small contribution towards that end by presenting a behavioral approach to benefits, with practical techniques to help HR practitioners improve the design, delivery, and evaluation of their programs. However, we still have a long way to go in applying the behavioral research, and in understanding the unique needs and circumstances of employees.

In this chapter, I'd like to offer a quick summary of the considerable territory we've covered thus far, and offer ideas on where behavioral science may take yet us.

A Different Way of Thinking About Benefits

This book starts with a premise: That employers can help employees take action on their benefits. Underlying that simple hopeful statement, there's an approach to thinking about benefits that is somewhat unusual.

In order for most benefit programs to work, employees must take action in some way — large or small. For health insurance offerings to be valuable, employees need to choose the right plan for themselves and their families. For an exercise program to be meaningful, employees need to exercise more than they otherwise would have. For a 401(k) program to deliver on its promise of retirement security, employees need to be engaged enough to customize their contributions and allocations to their own needs, even when auto-enrollment and auto-escalation are in place.

When employees don't take action on their benefits, that doesn't mean they are lazy or stupid. It means they — we — are only human. We all get distracted, discouraged, or overwhelmed. We all forget, procrastinate, or fail to act in our own long-term interest. The fact that the HR team is pouring its blood, sweat, and tears into designing programs that can *help* employees handle the challenges of life — medical expenses, retirement, etc. — doesn't change that basic fact that employees are only human. It's natural to become frustrated when employees clearly don't read announcements about their benefits, or fail to take advantage of good programs like 401(k)s and FSAs. But, there's a better response than frustration; that's to find a solution.

The solution requires a hard-nosed behavioral realism that can seem foreign to the spirit of HR: care and support employees, while balancing the needs of the company. A hard-nosed behavioral approach actually complements that spirit, and helps bring it to fruition. It starts with clear goals and metrics for any benefit program or communication, and then infuses those goals and metrics throughout the design, delivery, and evaluation of benefits. It means identifying the specific obstacles that employees face, rigorously analyzing whether vendor (and internal) programs will help employees overcome those obstacles, then putting in the time and energy required to help employees take action with the tools of behavioral science.

Focusing on behavior and outcomes doesn't necessarily mean being cold-hearted, however. Many companies rightfully see their benefits as tools to empower and enrich the lives of their employees. Others focus squarely on the bottom-line return on investment of their benefit programs, and the legal risks that need to be mitigated — does an HSA really decrease health costs, does the retirement package fulfill all of its legal mandates? Most companies think in terms of both sides. The behavioral approach to benefits presented here doesn't dictate what the company's goal should be — but rather that the goal should be clearly defined and pursued systematically.

Focusing on behavior and outcomes also shouldn't mean being manipulative or coercive. Employers have a responsibility — both legal and ethical — to deal with their employees justly. Throughout this book, I've tried to focus on situations in which employees want to take action, but struggle; situations in which a better-designed or delivered benefit program can help them pursue their own goals. Have no illusions though: Many of the techniques documented here have been used for unethical and murky purposes in the past; behavioral researchers are bringing them to the light so they can serve a more positive role as well.

Employers can help employees to take action in a non-coercive, empowering way in (at least) two situations. First, employers accidentally create barriers for employees that block them from using their benefits: Through email designs that evoke a strong negative reaction among employees, through benefits portals that are hard to understand and navigate, and through retirement plans that behavioral researchers have found to be overwhelming and lead to poor decisions. In part, this book is about how to identify and overcome these self-imposed obstacles. Removing employer-imposed obstacles is clearly empowering and non-coercive. Second, the book is also about helping employees overcome obstacles in their daily lives — based on the simple human limitations we all share — from limited attention to limited willpower or memory.

The Two Core Models

To help HR practitioners apply behavioral research to employee benefits, I've offered two core models: One for how employees decide about benefits, and one for how employers can apply behavioral methods throughout the benefits process.

CREATE

The CREATE funnel highlights the six things that occur if an employee is to take action on a benefit program:

❖ **Cue:** Something needs to cue the person to think about acting.

❖ **Reaction:** The mind automatically reacts intuitively and emotionally.

❖ **Evaluation.** With conscious awareness, the mind does a quick cost-benefit analysis.

❖ **Ability.** The person must actually be able to act and know it.

❖ **Time pressure.** The person needs to have a reason to act now.

❖ **Experience**. The person must generally have a good experience the first time, if they are ever going to (voluntarily) take action again.

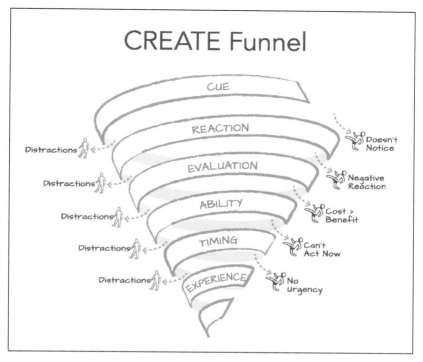

Figure 16: Six Obstacles to Behavior Change

Each one of these factors can become an obstacle, and block employees from taking action, even if they wanted to.

ACTION

The ACTION model shows how HR teams can complement their existing benefits design and delivery process with lessons from the behavioral sciences:

❖ **Analyze**: Figure out what employees need, given their existing benefits offerings, and the behavioral obstacles they face.

❖ **Craft:** Design benefits interventions that align employee and employer needs, and help employees actually take action to use them.

❖ **Test**: Test key assumptions about the intervention before implementing it in full, with a pilot program or a less formal trial.

❖ **Implement**: Implement the benefits intervention itself, tailoring communications carefully based on behavioral research.

❖ **Observe**: Assess the impact of the program with rigorous methods, especially randomized control trials.

❖ **Navigate:** Handle the inevitable challenges and find solutions; iteration is almost always required for effective behavior change.

You can visualize the approach as a benefits improvement cycle, as shown in Figure 17. The basic process is one familiar to HR professionals; in the details, however, new tools and resources are available that can improve the impact of HR's work.

Figure 17: Six Ways to Apply Behavioral Research to Benefits

A Vision of Partnerships

What does behavioral research mean for the future of benefits?

First, it means that in the future, we can better direct our attention to the real impact that benefit programs have on employees and companies. HR leaders shouldn't have to rely on industry-wide benchmarks to determine what their benefit offerings and design parameters should be. Similarly, leaders shouldn't have to rely on the number of people who merely "participate" in a program to tell if it is working or not.

Benchmarks and participation metrics are just proxies for what really matters — does a program serve the needs of employees and their company? Does it actually work? By developing rigorous metrics of the *outcomes* that programs generate, we will be able to move away from imperfect proxies.

Second, behavioral research means we can continue to systematically improve our impact. We can test our implicit assumptions about employee behavior and needs, and redesign our plans and our communications to better suit the realities of both. We can increase our bang for our buck — our impact on investment — over time.

In order to accomplish this, I envision a world of greater partnerships. First, I think we can have a deeper partnership between employees and HR. It's understandable, but unnecessary, that HR teams get frustrated at employee inaction on their benefits. Tools from behavioral science can help HR practitioners work with employees to better understand why employees struggle to take action, and help them overcome those obstacles — empowering employees, without trying to push them into something they don't want to do.

We can also have greater partnerships between employers and benefit providers. Tools from the behavioral sciences can help HR leaders hold their vendors accountable for the impact of their programs. They can also help vendors conduct the scientific testing they need to document the value of their programs and stand out among their competitors. Much of that scientific assessment can, and should, occur in partnership with their clients — it is often only the HR team that has access to the full suite of data about employee health, engagement, performance, and retention that are required for impact metrics.

I'll be the first to admit that this vision is a long way off. There's a tremendous amount that all of us can, and should, learn about the true behavioral impact of our benefit programs, and about how to best apply behavioral research. We've taken the first, exciting steps, and I look forward to what we will discover along the way.

APPENDIXES

GLOSSARY

Above the Fold: The part of a webpage or screen that a user first sees, without scrolling. Analogous to the top of a newspaper, which is visible when it is folded.

Behavioral Approach to Benefits: The core approach shown in this book, applying behavioral economics and psychology to the design and implementation of benefits packages. It is based on two principles:

Principle 1: Benefit Programs Depend On Behavior Change.

Principle 2: Behavior Change Requires Clear Goals & Metrics.

Benefits intervention: Any change to a benefit offering that has a behavioral impact; be it a new vendor program, a change to an existing one, an event, a communication around an event or program, etc.

Benefits intervention: Any change to a benefits package, whether it be adding a new program, changing the cost structure of an existing one, or better crafting the communications employees receive about their programs.

Behavioral Economics: An increasingly popular subfield of economics that studies the psychological and social causes of individual economic behavior.

Behavioral Science: A branch of science that focuses on and attempt to build generalizable models of human behavior. It historically covers psychology, sociology, and anthropology. Similar methods are also applied in behavioral economics and the behavioral political science. *See also: Behavioral Social Science.*

Behavioral Social Science: An umbrella term for the use of behavioral methods (including the focus on individual institutional behavior and the search for generalizable models based on observable real world factors) in the social sciences, especially in behavioral economics and behavioral political science.

Call to Action (CTA): What you are asking readers to do. Usually, this refers specifically to the text of the link or button in an email that asks readers to click. In a benefits context, it refers to the action that an internal communication requests — signing up for a benefit, attending a seminar, etc.

CHRO: Chief Human Resources Officer; head of the HR department.

CFO: Chief Financial Officer; head of the finance department.

Conversion Funnel: An illustration showing the portion of individuals who take each of a series of actions that lead up to a target outcome ("conversion" into a customer, etc.) A common term in marketing, here it is applied to the steps leading up to employees using their benefits.

Experimental Optimization: Using experiments to learn about what works with a (randomly selected) subset of employees, and then applying those lessons to rest of the employees. Ideally, this occurs as part of a staggered rollout in multiple waves — in the first wave, two or more ideas are tested out, in the second wave, the lessons from the prior wave are applied and a different set of ideas are tested, etc. *See also: Staggered Rollout RCT.*

Fail Fast: The philosophy that one should test assumptions early on, to pull inevitable problems from the future into the present. That allows you to fix them before they are expensive and embarrassing. The term is common in the Lean Startup community. *See also: Lean Startup.*

Impact of Investment, IOI: The net impact that a company generates from spending resources on a benefit program. In the behavioral approach to benefits, this term replaces ROI (or financial return) to indicate that a company may seek a financial or non-financial return on its investment, but it should still be rigorously tracked as with ROI. *See also: ROI.*

Lean Startup: A popular method for business and product development; coined in the book *The Lean Startup* by Eric Ries. The approach assumes that iteration is needed to develop a solid business and that with each iteration hypotheses about how customers and the business work should be tested. Here, we apply the concepts to testing assumptions about how employees will react to benefits.

Pre/Post Analysis: A simple analysis in which one compares outcomes of interest for a group of people before and after an event. For example, comparing the eating habits of employees before and after the rollout of a new wellness program. Unfortunately, this type of analysis does not control for other factors occurring at the same time — such as changes in diet because of the time of year.

Randomized Control Trial (a.k.a. RCT, A/B Test, Experiment): The gold standard for assessing causal impact of a program. When applied to benefits, some randomly selected employees receive the program on day one, and others don't. Then, the company tracks outcomes for the two groups, and compares them. The random assignment process controls allows the company to look squarely at the impact of the program itself, and factor out any other influences — like the demographics of the employees, their prior interest in the program, their current habits, etc. *See also: Staggered Rollout.*

Return on Investment, ROI: The rate of return on an investment, or net profit divided by total assets invested. In a benefits context, the term is applied to mean the financial benefit a company receives from spending resources on a benefit program. *See also: IOI.*

Staggered Rollout RCT: a type of experiment in which all employees receive a benefits intervention, but when they receive it is somehow randomized. For example, a selected randomly set of employees receive an email about a new benefit on day one, and the rest receive it at some later date. *See also: Randomized Control Trial (RCT).*

BIBLIOGRAPHY

Aargaard, Michel. 2013. "7 Universal Conversion Optimization Principles." http://contentverve.com/wp-content/uploads/2013/07/7-Universal-Conversion-Optimization-Principles.pdf.

Amabile, Teresa, and Steven Kramer. 2011. *The Progress Principle: Using Small Wins to Ignite Joy, Engagement, and Creativity at Work*. 1 edition. Boston, Mass: Harvard Business Review Press.

Anderson, Stephen P. 2011. *Seductive Interaction Design: Creating Playful, Fun, and Effective User Experiences*. Berkeley, CA: New Riders.

Ariely, Dan. 2008. *Predictably Irrational The Hidden Forces That Shape Our Decisions*. New York, NY: HarperCollins.

Ariely, Dan, George Loewenstein, and Drazen Prelec. 2003. "'Coherent Arbitrariness': Stable Demand Curves Without Stable Preferences." *The Quarterly Journal of Economics* 118 (1): 73–105.

Arnold, Chris. 2014. "How Do Companies Boost 401(k) Enrollment? Make It Automatic." *NPR.org*. Accessed August 6. http://www.npr.org/2014/04/21/303683792/how-do-companies-boost-401-k-enrollment-make-it-automatic.

Bakker, Arnold B., and Wilmar B. Schaufeli. 2010. "Defining and Measuring Work Engagement: Bringing Clarity to the Concept." In *Work Engagement: A Handbook of Essential Theory and Research. Bakker and Leiter Eds*. Psychology Press.

Balz, John, and Stephen Wendel. 2014. *Communicating for Behavior Change: Nudging Employees Through Better Emails*. HelloWallet.

Begley, Sharon. 2014. "PepsiCo's Workplace Wellness Program Fails the Bottom Line -Study." *Reuters*, January 7. http://www.reuters.com/article/2014/01/07/us-wellness-workplace-idUSBREA0510R20140107.

Benartzi, Shlomo, and Richard H Thaler. 2001. "Naive Diversification Strategies in Defined Contribution Saving Plans." *American Economic Review* 91 (1): 79–98.

Berman, Kristen, Dan Ariely, and Jason Hreha. 2014. *Hacking Human Nature for Good: A Practical Guide to Changing Human Behavior*.

Benz Communications. 2012. "Inside Benefits Communication Survey Report." http://www.benzcommunications.com/sites/default/files/wysiwyg/blog/Inside-Benefits-Communication-Survey-Report-2012.pdf.

Benz Communications. 2014. "Benefits Communication Master Class." http://www.benzcommunications.com/resources/benefits-communication-master-class-download.

bswift. 2014. *2014 Bswift Benefits Study*. bswift. http://www.bswift.com/?/public/industry-insights#2014-bswift-benefits-study.

Clear, James. 2014. "How Long Does it Actually Take to Form a New Habit?" *James Clear's Blog*. http://jamesclear.com/new-habit.

Corporate Leadership Council. 2004. "Driving Performance and Retention through Employee Engagement". Washington, DC: Corporate Executive Board. http://www.usc.edu/programs/cwfl/assets/pdf/Employee%20engagement.pdf.

Dean, Jeremy. 2013. *Making Habits, Breaking Habits: Why We Do Things, Why We Don't, and How to Make Any Change Stick*. Boston, MA, USA: Da Capo Press.

De Bono, Edward. 1973. *Lateral Thinking: Creativity Step by Step*. New York: Harper & Row.

Dicken, John E. 2008. "Health Savings Accounts: Participation Increased and Was More Common Among Individuals with Higher Incomes". GAO-08-474R. Washington, D.C.: United States Government Accountability Office. http://digitalcommons.ilr.cornell.edu/key_workplace/507.

Draaisma, Douwe. 2013. *Why Life Speeds Up As You Get Older*. Cambridge, UK: Cambridge University Press.

Duflo, Esther, William Gale, Jeffrey Liebman, Peter Orszag, and Emmanuel Saez. 2005. *Saving Incentives for Low- and Middle-Income Families: Evidence from a Field Experiment with H&R Block*. Working Paper 11680. National Bureau of Economic Research. http://www.nber.org/papers/w11680.

Fellowes, Matt, and Katy Willemin. 2013. *The Retirement Breach in Defined Contribution Plans*. HelloWallet Research Reports. http://signup.hellowallet.com/retirementbreach/.

Fogg, B. J., Jonathan Marshall, Othman Laraki, Alex Osipovich, Chris Varma, Nicholas Fang, Jyoti Paul, et al. 2001. "What Makes Web Sites Credible?: A Report on a Large Quantitative Study." In *Proceedings of the SIGCHI Conference on Human Factors in Computing Systems*, 61–68. CHI '01. New York, NY, USA: ACM.

Foster, Denise, Heidi tenBroek, and Sharon Stocker. 2014. "Effective Employee Communication: The Benefits of Best Practices." *Milliman*. Accessed January 3. /insight/eb/Effective-employee-communication-The-benefits-of-best-practices/.

Gallup. 2013a. "Engagement at Work: Its Effect on Performance Continues in Tough Economic Times." http://www.gallup.com/file/strategicconsulting/161459/2012%20 Q12%20Meta-Analysis%20Summary%20of%20Findings.pdf.

——. 2013b. "State of the American Workplace: Employee Engagement Insights for U.S. Business Leaders." http://www.gallup.com/strategicconsulting/163007/state-american-workplace.aspx.

——. 2014. "Gallup Employee Engagement Center." https://q12.gallup.com/.

Gladwell, Malcolm. 2005. *Blink: The Power of Thinking Without Thinking*. 1st ed. New York, NY: Little, Brown and Company.

Goel, Vindu. 2014. "Facebook Tinkers With Users' Emotions in News Feed Experiment, Stirring Outcry." *The New York Times*, June 29. http://www.nytimes.com/2014/06/30/technology/facebook-tinkers-with-users-emotions-in-news-feed-experiment-stirring-outcry.html.

Gollwitzer, Peter M. 1999. "Implementation Intentions: Strong Effects of Simple Plans." *American Psychologist* 54 (7): 493.

Hanoch, Yaniv, Thomas Rice, Janet Cummings, and Stacey Wood. 2009. "How Much Choice Is Too Much? The Case of the Medicare Prescription Drug Benefit." *Health Services Research* 44 (4): 1157–68.

Hamilton, Jon. 2008. "Think You're Multitasking? Think Again." *NPR.org*. Accessed 2014 May 8. http://www.npr.org/templates/story/story.php?storyId=95256794.

Harter, James K., Frank L. Schmidt, and Theodore L. Hayes. 2002. "Business-Unit-Level Relationship between Employee Satisfaction, Employee Engagement, and Business Outcomes: A Meta-Analysis." *Journal of Applied Psychology* 87 (2): 268.

Haupt, Angela. 2010. "Can Crash Diets Be a Good Way to Lose Weight?" *US News & World Report*. http://health.usnews.com/health-news/diet-fitness/diet/articles/2010/08/24/can-crash-diets-be-a-good-way-to-lose-weight.

Hern, Alex. 2014. "OKCupid: We Experiment on Users. Everyone Does." *The Guardian*, July 29, sec. Technology. http://www.theguardian.com/technology/2014/jul/29/okcupid-experiment-human-beings-dating.

Issenberg, Sasha. 2010. "How Behavioral Science Is Remaking Politics." *The New York Times*, October 29, sec. Magazine. http://www.nytimes.com/2010/10/31/magazine/31politics-t.html.

Iyengar, Sheena S, and M.R. Lepper. 2000. "When Choice Is Demotivating: Can One Desire Too Much of a Good Thing?" *Journal of Personality and Social Psychology* 79 (6): 995–1006.

Iyengar, Sheena S., Wei Jiang, and Gur Huberman. 2003. *How Much Choice Is Too Much? Contributions to 401 (k) Retirement Plans*. 2003-10. Pension Research Council Working Paper. http://www.archetype-

advisors.com/Images/Archetype/Participation/how%20much%20i
s%20too%20much.pdf.

Kahn, William A. 1992. "To Be Fully There: Psychological Presence at
Work." *Human Relations* 45 (4): 321–49.

Kahneman, Daniel. 2011. *Thinking, Fast and Slow*. 1st ed. New York, NY:
Farrar, Straus and Giroux.

Kahneman, Daniel, and Amos Tversky. 1984. "Choices, Values, and
Frames." *American Psychologist* 39 (4): 341.

Kane, Robert L., Paul E. Johnson, Robert J. Town, and Mary Butler. 2004.
"A Structured Review of the Effect of Economic Incentives on
Consumers' Preventive Behavior." *American Journal of Preventive
Medicine* 27 (4): 327–52. doi:10.1016/j.amepre.2004.07.002.

Karlan, Dean, Margaret McConnell, Sendhil Mullainathan, and Jonathan
Zinman. 2011. "Getting to the Top of Mind: How Reminders
Increase Saving". National Bureau of Economic Research Working
Paper no. 16205.

Kenexa. 2009. "The Impact of Employee Engagement."
http://www.kenexa.com/getattachment/8c36e336-3935-4406-8b7b-
777f1afaa57d/The-Impact-of-Employee-Engagement.aspx.

Kruse, Kevin. 2012. "What Is Employee Engagement." *Forbes*.
http://www.forbes.com/sites/kevinkruse/2012/06/22/employee-
engagement-what-and-why/.

Lally, Phillippa, Cornelia H. M. van Jaarsveld, Henry W. W. Potts, and Jane
Wardle. 2010. "How Are Habits Formed: Modelling Habit
Formation in the Real World." *European Journal of Social Psychology* 40
(6): 998–1009.

Lewis, Al. 2012. *Why Nobody Believes the Numbers: Distinguishing Fact from
Fiction in Population Health Management*. 1 edition. Hoboken, N.J:
Wiley.

Locke, Edwin A. 1976. "The Nature and Causes of Job Satisfaction." In
Handbook of Industrial and Organizational Psychology, M. D. Dunnette Ed.,
1297–134. Chicago: Rand McNally.

Lott, Maxim. 2013. "Gov't Knows Best? White House Creates 'Nudge
Squad' to Shape Behavior". *FoxNews.com*. July 30.
http://www.foxnews.com/politics/2013/07/30/govt-knows-best-
white-house-creates-nudge-squad-to-shape-behavior/.

Macey, William H., and Benjamin Schneider. 2008. "The Meaning of
Employee Engagement." *Industrial and Organizational Psychology* 1 (1):
3–30.

Madrian, Brigitte C. 2012. *Matching Contributions and Savings Outcomes: A
Behavioral Economics Perspective*. Working Paper 18220. National
Bureau of Economic Research.
http://www.nber.org/papers/w18220.

Madrian, Brigitte C., and Dennis F. Shea. 2001. "The Power of Suggestion:
Inertia in 401(k) Participation and Savings Behavior." *The Quarterly
Journal of Economics* 116 (4): 1149–87.

Mandell, Lewis, and Linda Schmid Klein. 2009. "The Impact of Financial Literacy Education on Subsequent Financial Behavior." *Journal of Financial Counseling and Planning* 20 (1): 15–24.

Marciano, Paul. 2010. *Carrots and Sticks Don't Work: Build a Culture of Employee Engagement with the Principles of RESPECT*. New York: McGraw-Hill.

Maslach, Christina, Wilmar B. Schaufeli, and Michael P. Leiter. 2001. "Job Burnout." *Annual Review of Psychology* 52 (1): 397–422.

Maurya, Ash. 2012. *Running Lean: Iterate from Plan A to a Plan That Works*. 2 edition. Sebastopol, CA: O'Reilly Media.

Mckenzie, Craig R.M, and Michael J Liersch. 2011. "Misunderstanding Savings Growth: Implications for Retirement Savings Behavior." *Journal of Marketing Research* 48 (SPL): S1–S13.

McKeown, Les. 2012. "A Very Simple Reason Employee Engagement Programs Don't Work." *Inc.com*. September 10. http://www.inc.com/les-mckeown/stop-employee-engagement-and-address-the-real-problem-.html.

Milkman, Katherine L., John Beshears, James J. Choi, David Laibson, and Brigitte C. Madrian. 2011. "Using Implementation Intentions Prompts to Enhance Influenza Vaccination Rates." *Proceedings of the National Academy of Sciences* 108 (26): 10415–20.

Miller, Jim. 2013. "Participant Education: Can It Really Work?" *DC Dimensions*. http://us.dimensional.com/pdf/dc_dimensions/2013summer/dcd_issue5_reprints_coverstory.pdf.

Mittal, Abhishek. 2011. "Employee Engagement Vs. Employee Satisfaction." *Mumblr*. http://abhishekmittal.com/2011/04/18/employee-engagement-vs-employee-satisfaction/.

Mullainathan, S, and E Shafir. 2009. "Savings Policy and Decision Making In Low-Income Households." *Insufficient Funds: Savings, Assets, Credit, and Banking among Low-Income Households*, 121.

Mullainathan, Sendhil, and Eldar Shafir. 2013. *Scarcity: Why Having Too Little Means So Much*. New York: Times Books.

Nessmith, William, Stephen Utkus, and Jean Young. 2007. *Measuring the Effectiveness of Automatic Enrollment*. https://institutional.vanguard.com/VGApp/iip/site/institutional/researchcommentary/article/EffectivenessAutoEnrollment.

Overly, Steven. 2014. "How to Ethically Test Customers in the Wake of Facebook's Lambasted Emotions Study." *The Washington Post*. 2014 July 4 http://www.washingtonpost.com/business/capitalbusiness/how-to-ethically-test-customers-in-the-wake-of-facebooks-lambasted-emotions-study/2014/07/03/902b9c54-02e8-11e4-8fd0-3a663dfa68ac_story.html.

Pappas, Stephanie. 2010. "'The Biggest Loser' Has Big Problems, Health Experts Say." *LiveScience.com*. http://www.livescience.com/9820-biggest-loser-big-problems-health-experts.html.

Podsakoff, Philip M., Scott B. MacKenzie, Jeong-Yeon Lee, and Nathan P. Podsakoff. 2003. "Common Method Biases in Behavioral Research: A Critical Review of the Literature and Recommended Remedies." *Journal of Applied Psychology* 88 (5): 879.

Ries, Eric. 2011. *The Lean Startup: How Today's Entrepreneurs Use Continuous Innovation to Create Radically Successful Businesses*. New York: Crown Business.

Robinson, D, S. Perryman, and S Hayday. 2004. "The Drivers of Employee Engagement". 408. Institute for Employee Studies.

Rudder, Christian. 2014. "We Experiment On Human Beings!" 2014. *OkTrends Blog*. Accessed 2014 August 6. http://blog.okcupid.com/index.php/we-experiment-on-human-beings.

Saks, Alan M. 2006. "Antecedents and Consequences of Employee Engagement." *Journal of Managerial Psychology* 21 (7): 600–619.

Schaufeli, Wilmar. 2014. "Tests." *Website of Wilmar Schaufeli*. http://www.wilmarschaufeli.nl/downloads/test-manuals/.

Schaufeli, Wilmar B., Arnold B. Bakker, and Marisa Salanova. 2006. "The Measurement of Work Engagement With a Short Questionnaire A Cross-National Study." *Educational and Psychological Measurement* 66 (4): 701–16.

Scheibehenne, Benjamin, Rainer Greifeneder, and Peter M. Todd. 2010. "Can There Ever Be Too Many Options? A Meta-Analytic Review of Choice Overload." *Journal of Consumer Research* 37 (3): 409–25.

Schwarz, Norbert, and Gerald L. Clore. 1983. "Mood, Misattribution, and Judgments of Well-Being: Informative and Directive Functions of Affective States." *Journal of Personality and Social Psychology* 45 (3): 513–23.

Sepah, Cameron. 2014. Phone Interview on Behavioral Science and Employee Benefits.

Sharpe, Lindsey. 2013. "U.S. Obesity Rate Climbing in 2013." *Gallup Well-Being*. http://www.gallup.com/poll/165671/obesity-rate-climbing-2013.aspx.

Shunk, Charles. 2009a. "VIDEO: Fun Theory Part 2 - VW Makes Throwing Stuff Away Fun." *Autoblog*. http://www.autoblog.com/2009/10/14/video-fun-theory-part-2-vw-makes-throwing-stuff-away-fun/.

———. 2009b. "VIDEO: Volkswagen Wants You to Have Fun... Taking the Stairs." *Autoblog*. http://www.autoblog.com/2009/10/08/video-volkswagen-wants-you-to-have-fun-taking-the-stairs/.

Stonehouse, Andy. 2013. "HSA Participation Prompts Higher Employee Engagement." *Benefit News*. December 13. http://ebn.benefitnews.com/news/hsa-participation-prompts-higher-employee-engagement-2738110-1.html.

Subramanian, Courtney. 2014. "'Nudge' Back in Fashion at White House." *Time*. Accessed May 9. http://swampland.time.com/2013/08/09/nudge-back-in-fashion-at-white-house/.

Thaler, Richard H., and Shlomo Benartzi. 2004. "Save More Tomorrow™: Using Behavioral Economics to Increase Employee Saving." *Journal of Political Economy* 112 (S1): S164–S187.

Thaler, Richard H., and Cass R. Sunstein. 2008. *Nudge: Improving Decisions about Health, Wealth, and Happiness*. New Haven, Connecticut: Yale Univ Press.

Thompson, Derek. 2013. "More Is More: Why the Paradox of Choice Might Be a Myth." *The Atlantic*. http://www.theatlantic.com/business/archive/2013/08/more-is-more-why-the-paradox-of-choice-might-be-a-myth/278658/.

Tufano, Peter. 2008. "Saving Whilst Gambling: An Empirical Analysis of UK Premium Bonds." *American Economic Review* 98 (2): 321–26.

Tversky, Amos, and Daniel Kahneman. 1974. "Judgment under Uncertainty: Heuristics and Biases." *Science*. 185 (4157): 1124-1131.

Tversky, Amos, and Daniel Kahneman. 1973. "Availability: A Heuristic for Judging Frequency and Probability." *Cognitive Psychology* 5 (2): 207–32.

Utkus, Stephen. 2014. Phone Interview on Behavioral Science and Employee Benefits.

Vanguard. 2013. "How America Saves." https://pressroom.vanguard.com/nonindexed/2013.06.03_How_America_Saves_2013.pdf.

Volpp, Kevin, and David Asch. 2014. "A Rapid Cycle Approach to Improving Medication Adherence Through Incentives and Remote Monitoring for Coronary Artery Disease Patients." *Penn LDI CHIBE | A Rapid Cycle Approach to Improving Medication Adherence Through Incentives and Remote Monitoring for Coronary Artery Disease Patients*.

Volpp KG, John LK, Troxel AB, Norton L, Fassbender J, and Loewenstein G. 2008. "Financial Incentive–based Approaches for Weight Loss: A Randomized Trial." *JAMA* 300 (22): 2631–37.

Wansink, Brian. 2010. *Mindless Eating: Why We Eat More than We Think*. New York: Bantam Books.

Weiss, Howard M. 2002. "Deconstructing Job Satisfaction: Separating Evaluations, Beliefs and Affective Experiences." *Human Resource Management Review* 12 (2): 173–94.

White, Philip. 2014. Phone Interview on Behavioral Science and Employee Benefits.

Willis, Janine, and Alexander Todorov. 2006. "First Impressions Making Up Your Mind After a 100-Ms Exposure to a Face." *Psychological Science* 17 (7): 592–98.

Wilson, Jacque, and Ashley Hayes. 2014. "'Biggest Loser' Winner: Too Thin?" *CNN*. http://www.cnn.com/2014/02/05/health/biggest-weight-loss/index.html.

Wilson, Timothy D. 2002. *Strangers to Ourselves: Discovering the Adaptive Unconscious*. Cambridge, Mass: Belknap Press.

Wood, Wendy, and David T. Neal. 2007. "A New Look at Habits and the Habit-Goal Interface." *Psychological Review* 114 (4): 843–63.

Wood, Wendy, Jeffrey M. Quinn, and Deborah A. Kashy. 2002. "Habits in Everyday Life: Thought, Emotion, and Action." *Journal of Personality and Social Psychology* 83 (6): 1281–97.

WorldAtWork. 2007. *The WorldatWork Handbook of Compensation, Benefits & Total Rewards: A Comprehensive Guide for HR Professionals*. 1 edition. Hoboken, N.J: Wiley.

Xerox HR Solutions. 2013. "BenefitWallet™ 2013 Member Survey Report." https://mybenefitwallet.com/CMS/portal/default/2013_BenefitWalletMemberSurvey.html.

ABOUT THE AUTHOR

Stephen is the Principal Scientist at HelloWallet, where he's worked for five years to develop applications that help users take control of their finances. He is a behavioral social scientist by training, and works with behavior economists and psychologists to conduct research on behavior change, especially around savings and spending behavior.

Stephen recently authored the book, *Designing for Behavior Change*, for O'Reilly Media that describes a step-by-step approach to applying behavioral economics to products that help people change their daily routines and behavior. He is the founder of Action Design Network, which hosts a conference and event series in four cities, serving over 1900 practitioners and researchers — people who build products to help users take action via behavioral techniques.

He lives near Washington DC with his wife, a newborn, and a really fun little three year old.

Made in the USA
Lexington, KY
08 June 2015